Effective Flex & Bison

Chris L. verBurg

Preface

When I started this book project, I had two goals. The first was to update the classic *Lex & Yacc* text (whose latest edition had been published in 1992) and focus it specifically on Flex and Bison. The second was to extend it to include usage tips similar to what Scott Meyer does in *Effective C++*.

In 2009, David Levine wrote an update to *Lex & Yacc*, focusing on Flex and Bison. *Flex & Bison* is a fantastic book: it not only bridges the seventeen-year gap in literature, but also its examples are far more relevant. It is a great read and I recommend it as the most important step to learning Flex and Bison.

However, *Flex & Bison* does not directly address my second goal, which was to include power-user tips. To that end, this book contains usage tips from a variety of sources and empirical results from my own experiments. It is my hope that this book helps you become a better Flex/Bison user.

This book assumes you have at least some experience with Flex and Bison. It does not assume you know any compiler theory.

Why write this book?

It is valid to ask why this book should be written, because there are several very good reasons why it should not:

• Since there is already a *Flex & Bison* book, in addition to their comprehensive documentation, won't this be redundant?

• Since Flex and Bison are old, won't the content already be obsolete?

• Since Flex and Bison are seldom used, is there any audience for it?

I have used Flex and Bison for several projects, and, as is the case with any third-party software, I have had questions about various issues that came up. The obvious resource is the internet, but it turned out not to be much help: searching for "lex" and "yacc" usually gives you web forums where someone posts a question that is never answered. Searching for "flex" and "bison" is worse: they turn up pages about Adobe (or Ford) Flex, and buffalo. The material in this book is not entirely redundant, though you will obviously find points that are mentioned elsewhere.

It is true that the use of Flex and Bison has been declining over the years. Their original purpose (creating compilers) was a big deal around 1980 when the number of computer languages was exploding, but that is less of a concern now. Their secondary use (general data file parsing) has been supplanted partly by newer parsing tools (re2c & lemon, ANTLR) but more so by data file standardization such as XML, JSON, and YAML. Still, Flex and Bison continue to live on. Having been introduced in the 1980s, they have more momentum than any other parsing tools, so there is generally more code written for them than the others. Much of the time, they remain the path of least resistance.

That said, it is certainly true that there are newer (and usually better) parsers available. re2c (Regular Expression 2 C) and Lemon work together very nicely and have much nicer input file formats. ANTLR combines

lexing and parsing into a single tool, is highly
sophisticated, and is actively maintained by a parsing-
theory professor. More significant is that those tools are all
thread safe. Thread safety is becoming a dominant factor
in software design: as microprocessor chips start holding
an increasing number of processor cores, software will be
able to use threading not only to sidestep I/O-bound
operations but also to truly execute code in parallel. Flex
and Bison come from the era of single-core processors,
when it was safe to communicate via global variables,
which presents an obstacle to threading.

However, nothing is a definitive win over Flex/
Bison. re2c does not have start states, so developers must
use Lemon's undocumented %fallback feature for
context-sensitive lexing (and even then I have found it
does not work reliably). Lemon is not a standalone project
but rather part of the sqlite project; as such, it is not really
actively maintained, and it is deplorably under-
documented. ANTLR's learning curve is huge, and has
scaling concerns due to it lexing all of the input before
starting any parsing.

Other resources

There are many resources for Flex and Bison (and
parsing theory), and I recognize the need to get a second
opinion on something that does not make sense. Here are a
few other places you can look:

- Bison's documentation is fantastic: http://
www.gnu.org/software/bison/manual/
bison.html
- Flex's documentation is also very good:
http://westes.github.io/flex/manual/
- *Lex & Yacc*, second edition, by Doug Brown

(1992). This is the classic text.

• *Flex & Bison*, first edition, by David Levine (2009). The update of the classic text.

• *Compilers: Principles, Techniques, & Tools*, by Aho et al (2007). This is the "dragon book". It has a comprehensive, dry explanation of parsing theory, which is sure to give any past CS student nightmarish flashbacks.

The examples in this book were compiled using the latest versions of Flex and Bison, which, as of this writing in late 2017, are:

- Flex: 2.6.4 (2017/05/06)
- Bison: 3.0.4 (2015/01/23)

I have intentionally not ripped apart the source code to either Flex or Bison for this book, and the reason is because I do not want to convey any internal information that might not exist in future versions. Things like `yyr1`, `yytrule`, and `yyn` are internal variables that can be used to construct the name of the current rule (great for debugging!), but there is no guarantee they will be available in future versions of Bison. Additionally, I have also tried to avoid any features that are currently marked as "experimental", such as Bison's delicious `%define parse.error verbose`.

Acknowledgements

First and foremost I have to express my appreciation for John Levine, not only for writing the O'Reilly *Flex & Bison* book (2009) but also for staying active on the Flex and Bison mailing lists.

For the basic idea behind getting `%locations` working (§3.2.5), I credit Brent Royal-Gordon for developing this solution in a stackoverflow post.

For the code snippets that eventually got `readline` working (§3.2.7), I thank Philip Herron and John Levine.

For the clever idea for testing isolated rules (§3.6.4), I credit Joel E. Denny.

Finally, for nothing in particular, I would like to also recognize Akim Demaille for managing Bison releases and staying active on the mailing list.

Chapter 1: Defining "Effective"

To say that something is effective is to say that it does what it set out to do (literally, that it has its intended effect). In the software world, there is a surprising number of intended effects other than the conversion of input to correct output. In many cases, software constraints contradict each other, and our role as developers and engineers is to decide between tradeoffs.

The idea of effectiveness extends past the final software product and into the software development process. Consider several stages of the software lifecycle:
- requirements gathering (what does the system need to do?)
- analysis (creating a solution in the user's domain)
- design (mapping the user's solution to the programmer's domain)
- implementation (actual programming)
- maintenance (new features, bug fixes)

In differing forms, effectiveness applies to all of these stages. The process suggestions in this book are mostly concerned with the design, implementation, and maintenance stages.

The following aspects of effectiveness are the ones most relevant to Flex/Bison applications. They guided the selection and refinement of the tips in this book. Note that there is some overlap between the criteria I have selected; for example, error checking falls in to just about every one of these categories.

Correctness

Correctness is the most important aspect of software, even more than speed. (As the proverb goes, speed gets you nowhere if you are headed the wrong way.) For Flex/Bison applications, what best practices ensure that our lexing and parsing are correct?

I will mention an important exception to parser correctness: in some cases, it is desirable to allow extra "illegal" syntax. Sometimes, by relaxing a strict requirement of the language, we can make the parser smaller, faster, easier to read, or easier to implement. (Specifically, see §3.6.2 about how *not* to handle a list of unordered parameters.)

Efficiency

Efficiency is the measure of resources consumed to perform some task. For software, that means the runtime and memory footprints; obviously we want our parsers to run as fast as possible, and consume as little memory as possible.

However, "time" also includes development time. How long does it take to finally figure out the right syntax in Flex to accept the intended pattern? How long does it take to resolve the conflicts in a Bison grammar? How much time does it take to update existing code with new features or bug fixes?

Programmers measure efficiency in terms of how long it takes to make the correct change to the code. That measure is intentionally broad so that it includes the time spent in each of the software process phases:

- learning how the existing code works
- figuring out how to make the change
- making the code
- testing the change

Robustness

Robustness is the ability to gracefully handle unexpected input. This is a significant topic for parsers because parsers are the front line of code encountering raw user input. Well done error handling is the difference between enabling the user to fix their own problems versus forcing them to research a cryptic message (or segfault, or other failure).

Some specific considerations for robustness:
- If an error is not fatal, does your program continue?
- Does your program catch all errors, or stop on the first one? If you halt on the first one, the user has to rerun after every fix to find the next one.
- Are errors reported helpfully? They should include all the information the user needs to know in order to resolve the issue, such as the file and line number, why the error is a problem, and perhaps even some suggested next steps.
- If the parser aborts, can it be re-invoked? Flex and Bison carry around some state that must be manually reset.

While *robustness* addresses errors due to bad input, *fault-tolerant* software can survive system errors such as network outages and filled disks. In practice, there are only a few places in Flex/Bison applications where you can improve your fault tolerance:

• Checking calls to `malloc` so that you know when you run out of memory
• Checking I/O operations, such as `fopen` and `fread`.

System errors like these are much rarer than other kinds of errors, and so programmers get in the lazy habit of not checking for them. When they do occur, they tend to materialize in ways that are obscure to everyone. It is essential to make sure every error message indicates exactly what is wrong. If possible, also include why the error occurred and what the user can do to fix it. Get in the habit of checking for system errors and reporting them coherently, before something downstream crashes and reports it incoherently.

Complexity

Complexity is the measure of how complicated the software is, which is important in at least two contexts: the ability to understand the code, and the ability to write tests for it. Understanding the code is obviously important for updating it, but remember the rule of thumb for short-term memory: after six months, your code might as well have been written by someone else.

For testing, it is easier to test a lot of small functions than to test a few big ones, because testing complexity is directly related to the number of branch paths.

It is immediately obvious when a grammar or a list of regular expressions becomes complex, because you find you can no longer understand it at a glance.

Maintainability

Maintainability refers to the ability to quickly understand, modify, and verify changes to software. Maintainability is greatly dependent on complexity. Numbers vary, but I have heard it said that up to 90% of the total time spent on any piece of production code is done after it has been initially deployed. Even without such a drastic extreme, time spent upfront to minimize maintenance effort is well invested.

Many activities fall in the category of "maintenance": fixing a bug, adding new functionality, refactoring, or porting to a new platform. Each of these can be made easier or harder by earlier design decisions. Not everyone agrees, but I have always found it better to prioritize maintenance time over run time; computers get faster with every release, but programmers do not.

Usability

Finally, usability is the qualification of how nice the software is to its users. For Flex/Bison, there are several layers of users. The first is the code that invokes your parser; many times this is also your code, but not always. Do you provide a consistent, helpful API? The second layer of users is the end user who invokes the parser with their input. Do they have any chance of deciphering your error messages?

Obviously, high usability is great for the users, but it also has a direct benefit to the programmer: it is easier to test. First, highly usable applications have a well-defined interface with clear expectations, which makes test development easier. Second, when a test fails, highly usable code will make it easy to track down the source of the problem.

I stress again the benefits of helpful error messages. An ideal error message conveys the problem (and possible solutions) in the user's domain, helping them fix it on their own. Without sufficient information to make progress, they will have to take up your time to discover their next steps.

Chapter 2: Flex

2.1 Core Flex Skills

2.1.1 Understanding token values

Flex and Bison allow you to associate values (such as 13 or "foo!") with tokens (such as NUMBER or STRING). While some tokens do not have an associated value (e.g. parentheses, operators such as +), values are essential for others. These values are consumed only by user code; Bison merely passes them along while using the tokens for parsing. There are two aspects of token values to understand in order to use them effectively: how to control their datatypes, and how they are passed between Flex and Bison.

The datatype for token values is defined in a global macro named YYSTYPE. Its default is int, which is great for NUMBER but useless for STRING. You could redefine it to be char*, and then it would be great for STRING but useless for NUMBER. Ultimately, you need a single datatype that could be either an int or a char* (or a float, or a pointer to an abstract syntax tree node, etc), and C's answer to that problem is a union. Thus, the typical parser will define YYSTYPE using Bison's %union directive. For example:

```
%union {
  int ival;
  float fval;
  char *sval;
  struct ASTNode *nval;
}
```

In the generated tab.h file, this example is turned

into the following C code (I removed some #line macros that are not relevant):

```
union YYSTYPE
{
    int ival;
    float fval;
    char *sval;
    struct ASTNode *nval;
};
```

The next important piece to understand is how Flex and Bison communicate token values. C does not allow a function to return more than one object, so yylex has to jump a hurdle to return both a token and its value to Bison. The solution is to put the token *number* in yylex's return value (tokens are just #define'd integers), and to put the token *value* in the global variable yylval (which is just an instance of the YYSTYPE that we redefined with %union). Thus a lexer would return a NUMBER token with something like this:

```
[0-9]+    {
    yylval.ival = atoi(yytext);
    return NUMBER;
}
```

Bison takes the value of yylval and adds it to its internal token value stack, and returns it back to you whenever a Bison rule references it (via $1, $2, etc). This brings us to the last important piece of information — Bison copies yylval by value, and pointers to global variables have to be handled carefully. Specifically, for the above example to handle strings correctly, it cannot merely set yylval.sval to yytext, because yytext is overwritten on every token. Some method of copying strings is required, such as:

8

```
[a-zA-Z]+    {
    yylval.sval = strdup(yytext);
    return STRING;
}
```

Finally, remember to avoid a corresponding memory leak. When Bison consumes the token value in a rule, it should either `free` it or pass ownership of the string to a datastructure that will `free` it later.

2.1.2 Understanding start-states

When you[1] call `yylex` to fetch the next token, it has a set of patterns that it tries to match. Usually, every pattern in your lexer is a candidate, but start-states give you runtime control over the set of patterns that should be considered.

One use for this mechanism is when tokens temporarily do not mean what they usually mean, such as in code comments. Most of a C file is numbers and variables and operators, but inside of a comment those are all meaningless; all you really care about is the end-of-comment marker. Thus, instead of all the normal C-language token patterns, you could establish a start state for comments that recognizes only two patterns: the end-of-comment marker, and *other*.[2]

Another use for start-states is to give the parser some control over the lexer, such as in version strings. Version strings are fundamentally strings (e.g. "1.2.3-4.5.6") but they sometimes look just like numbers (e.g. "1.2"). If you have written your patterns correctly, you listed your number pattern before your string pattern, which then exposes a problem: the "1.2" is parsed as a number instead of as a string, and manifests as a parse error. We could use a start-state here to force Flex to parse the next thing it sees as a string.

Start states can be either *exclusive* or *non-exclusive*. Both will match the patterns in that state, but the difference is that *non-exclusive* states will also match

---

[1] Where by "you" I mean `yyparse`, usually.

[2] Note that this is not the best way to handle block comments; see §2.2.1.

patterns in *no* state. An illustrative example is whitespace, which typically has the exact same pattern everywhere — you could define it without a start-state, and then your non-exclusive start-states automatically pick it up without having to duplicate it. Our second example (forcing version numbers into strings) would do this, which is good because it automatically allows arbitrary whitespace around the version string. However, our second example (comments) would not do this, because it does not care about matching whitespace. A comment start-state would then be *exclusive*. Putting all of this into one contrived example:

```
%s FORCE_STRING
%x COMMENT

%%

[ \t]+    {
    // Ignore whitespace.
}
<FORCE_STRING>[a-zA-Z0-9\.]+  {
    // Whether or not this looks like a
    // number, return it as a string.
    ...
    return STRING;
}
[0-9]+\.[0-9]+  {
    // Normal number.  Listed after
    // <FORCE_STRING> to lower
    // precedence.
    ...
}
VERSION  {
    // Start of a VERSION declaration.
    BEGIN(FORCE_STRING);
    ...
}
```

```
[a-zA-Z0-9\.]+  {
    // Normal string.  Listed after
    // both <FORCE_STRING> and VERSION
    // to lower precedence.
    ...
}
"/*"  {
    // Start of a comment.
    BEGIN(COMMENT);
}
<COMMENT>"*/"  {
    // End of comment - go back to
    // regular lexing.
    BEGIN(INITIAL);
}
<COMMENT>.  {
    // Ignore everything else while
    // we are in a comment.
}
```

2.1.3 Using start-state stacks

Flex stores the current start-state in a global integer variable[3], and the `BEGIN` macro merely updates it. While this mechanism is straightforward for implementing "go to state named FOO", it is clunky for implementing "go back to previous state". Reusing §2.1.2's examples, you want to be able to process comments regardless of which start-state the lexer happens to be in at the moment, so the `BEGIN(INITIAL)` at the end of comments is actually wrong. Specifically, what if there is a comment in the middle of a version string, such as:

```
VERSION /* hi mom */ 3.14
```

Here we see `VERSION` and go into the `FORCE_STRING` state, and then see `/*` and go into the `COMMENT` state. When we see the closing `*/`, we actually want to go back to `FORCE_STRING`, not to `INITIAL`.

In general, we could have an arbitrary number of start-states nested like this. Flex's solution to this situation is a dedicated stack for start-states. (Aside: from a theory standpoint, using a stack upgrades Flex from understanding *regular expressions* to understanding *push-down automata*, which is a step up in computational power. For example, you could use the start-state stack to match opening and closing parentheses, something you cannot do with Flex alone. You may find cases where Flex is enough to solve a complete parsing problem without having to use Bison at all!)

In practice, to leverage the start-state stack, lexers should use `yy_push_state` and `yy_pop_state` instead

---

[3] `YY_START`, if you are curious.

of BEGIN. Enabling those functions requires `%option stack`, so our upgraded comment-handling example looks like this:

```
%option stack

%x COMMENT

%%

"/*" {
    // Start of a comment.
    yy_push_state(COMMENT);
 }
<COMMENT>"*/" {
    // End of comment - go back to
    // the previous state.
    yy_pop_state();
 }
<COMMENT>. {
    // Ignore everything else while
    // we are in a comment.
 }
```

We will see start-state stacks again when we cover handling #include-like mechanisms in §2.4.7.

2.1.4 Reporting errors

Reporting errors from Flex is a little tricky. There is no way to control the return code from `yylex` because the return code is semantically interpreted as a token number, which could be anything. If you are generating C code (instead of C++ or Java), then you do not have exceptions. Your best option[4] is a hard-stop via `exit` or `abort`.

Flex has a built-in function to handle this for you: `yy_fatal_error`. It accepts one parameter (a `char*`), echoes it to stderr, and then calls `exit(2)`[5].

`yy_fatal_error` has at least two shortcomings that may compel you to replace it with your own function. First, since it calls `exit` right away, your application will stop after the first error, as opposed to reporting the first N problems before halting. You may decide that this is not acceptable.

However, a worse problem is that `yy_fatal_error` is not a drop-in replacement for `printf`. Specifically, you cannot include variables in the string you pass to it. In order to avoid error messages that are unhelpfully vague ("could not open a file" or "found an unexpected character"), you will have to do some string formatting on your own. The minimal implementation uses `asprintf`:

---

[4] Note that *best* does not always imply *good*.

[5] Technically it calls `exit(YY_EXIT_FAILURE)`, so that you could re-#`define YY_EXIT_FAILURE` to any number you want.

```
// Encountered error:
char *errstr;
asprintf(&errstr, "ERROR, line %d: could
not open file %s",
   yylineno, myfile);
yy_fatal_error(errstr);
```

Here is a suggested error function for Flex, which will allow up to, oh, 10 errors before halting, and looks more like printf:

```
%{
#include <stdarg.h>
void myerror(const char*, ...);
%}
%%
...
%%
static int NUM_ERRORS = 0;
void myerror(const char *format, ...) {
  va_list args;
  va_start(args, format);

  vfprintf(stderr, format, args);

  va_end(args);

  ++NUM_ERRORS;
  if (NUM_ERRORS == 10) {
    exit(YY_EXIT_FAILURE);
  }
  return;
}
```

Note that the ellipses in this code segment are actually three periods that go into the source code, unlike the other ellipses in this book that mean "your code goes here".

Do not forget to check NUM_ERRORS after invoking yyparse (or yylex) so that you can still abort when there are fewer than N errors.

If you need Flex to not issue a hard-stop with exit, you could replace it with a call to yyterminate to cease processing any more input. However, yyterminate will not invoke any <<EOF>> rules, so be careful if you have a buffer stack.

See also §3.4.1 for a related discussion on yyerror, which you could possibly share between Flex and Bison.

2.1.5 Lexing binary input

Handling binary input is, in theory, not so different from handling text input, especially when you consider that Flex is just a state machine operating on each character of the input. Two interesting possible applications for reading binary data are databases and unicode[6].

The syntax for matching a binary character is mostly straightforward — simply backslash the numeric value you want to match. They are treated like any other character, and you can even use them in compound matches and character ranges. For example, the following are equivalent (assuming ASCII encoding):

```
[a-zA-Z]+ { ... }

[\x61-\x7a\x41-\x5a]+ { ... }
```

Notice that we specified the numeric character values in hexadecimal. It turns out, oddly, that Flex recognizes only octal and hexadecimal. The x after the backslash above indicates this is a hex number; without it, Flex assumes it is an octal number, which is rather unintuitive to anyone inheriting your code, so I advise avoiding octal specifications.

Lexing binary input has an impact on table compression. Flex's default behavior is to generate an 8-bit scanner, but since enabling -Cf or -CF for speed explodes the sizes of the tables, Flex tries to save you half the space by switching to a 7-bit scanner. However, you need all 8 bits for binary input. Thus, if you have enabled either -Cf

---

[6] Flex itself does not support unicode (that is, using unicode characters in patterns is asking for trouble), but it can be used to lex unicode input.

or -CF, you will usually need to force Flex back to an 8-bit scanner with %option 8bit. Fortunately, Flex will recognize this situation and issue you a helpful error:

```
flex: scanner requires -8 flag to use
the character ...
```

A final caveat on zero ("0") bytes. Matching a literal zero works just fine in Flex (that is, input does not mistakenly see it as the end of the file), but all of the normal string functions would see it as the end of a string. Thus, your code *will* have to rely on yyleng when dealing with yytext. Here is an example custom replacement for strdup:

```
%{
char* my_binary_strdup();
%}
%%
[a-zA-Z\x00]+   {
    yylval = my_binary_strdup();
    return STRING;
  }
%%
char* my_binary_strdup() {
  char *res = malloc(yyleng);
  int i;
  for (i = 0; i < yyleng; ++i) {
    res[i] = yytext[i];
  }
  return res;
}
```

Note some key differences between this and the example in a later tip (§2.2.4) where we make another custom strdup replacement:

• In addition to avoiding strdup, we have to avoid using the values in yytext at all. We have no choice but to iterate between 0 and `yyleng`.

 • We allocate `yyleng` bytes instead of `yyleng+1`, because presumably binary data that could include zero bytes would not try to use one as an end-of-string marker.

Finally, since the consumer cannot use `strlen`, it will need to be told how long the binary string is. A custom `struct` for bundling the data and the string length is almost certainly required.

2.1.6 C++

There are two ways to "support" C++ in Flex - the first is to have it generate normal C code but then compile and link it with other C++ code; the second way is to have Flex generate actual C++ code.

Compiling and linking Flex's generated C code with C++ is fully supported, and you should have no problems including C++ code in user actions. However, there are still the usual concerns with mixing C and C++ code and compilers. First is that Flex will continue to use `malloc` and `free` internally, and those chunks of memory should not be mixed with calls to `new` and `delete`. The particular dangers are:

- `YY_BUFFER_STATE` objects and character buffers created by `yy_create_buffer`, `yy_scan_buffer`, and `yy_scan_bytes`; but you should be using `yy_delete_buffer` to free up that memory.
- the buffer stack updated by `yypush_buffer_state` and `yypop_buffer_state`; but you should be using `yylex_destroy` to free its memory.
- `yytext`. You never own this and should not be trying to allocate or free it in any way. However, you should be copying it for string values, and then you should give some thought to allocation. Fortunately, Flex does not care how you copy `yytext`, so you can use `malloc`, `std::string`, or anything else you like.

Similarly, Flex will continue to use C's file functions instead of C++'s streams. `yyin` will still be a pointer to a `FILE`, so even if the rest of your action code is C++, you will still need to use `fopen` et al when switching input files.

Remember that using C functions in code compiled with a C++ compiler requires you to update your #includes. For example, #include <stdlib.h> becomes #include <cstdlib>.

Another consideration is linkage between C-compiled files and C++-compiled files. Specifically, if you want to compile the lexer in C but include it in a C++ project, any lexer declarations in the C++ code will have to specify C linkage in order to survive name mangling. yylex is the most obviously affected point of visibility, but depending on your setup you may also need it for yytext, your error function(s), and anything else that requires visibility:

```
extern "C" int yylex();
```

Finally, when compiling from C++, Flex's input is renamed to yyinput to avoid a conflict with the C++ stream of the same name, and yywrap is declared with C linkage.

Suppose, however, you want Flex to generate actual C++ code. Flex has tried to add support for that, and many people have put in a lot of effort to get it working as well as possible. However, as of this writing (late 2017), even the documentation warns about it:

```
IMPORTANT: the present form of the
scanning class is experimental and may
change considerably between major
releases.
```

The generated code itself has further admonitions:

```
The c++ scanner is a mess. The
```

```
FlexLexer.h header file relies on the
following macro. This is required in
order to pass the c++-multiple-scanners
test in the regression suite. We get
reports that it breaks inheritance. We
will address this in a future release of
flex, or omit the C++ scanner
altogether.
```

I could not get even a simple "hello world" lexer to compile on my system; apparently my FlexLexer.h[7] is incompatible with my version of Flex (2.6.4). Check the latest Flex documentation and see if you have more luck on your platform than I did.

---

[7] Xcode version 6.0.1

2.2 Efficiency

2.2.1 Handling block comments

New Flex/Bison users are always tempted to match block comments (such as C's /* .. */) with a Flex pattern such as the following:

```
/\*.*\*/   ;
```

While (almost) academically ideal, this is horrendous for several reasons. First, . does not match carriage returns, so this fails on multi-line comments. You would have to solve this problem by upgrading it to include \n, e.g.:

```
/\*[.\n]*\*/   ;
```

Second, Flex stores all text it matches in a buffer, used or not. This means the Flex memory footprint for this pattern depends on the size of the largest comment in your input! Additionally, if it is large enough to trigger a resizing of Flex's buffer, it has to rescan the pattern from the beginning, which adds a performance penalty to comments.

Third, * is a greedy match, so it will scan right past the first */ in order to see if there is another one farther on. If there is, then any non-comment section between two block comments is erroneously considered part of the comment and dropped.

Finally, this pattern does not let you maintain the current line number easily, since it absorbs carriage returns in the text.

A common next attempt is to use start-states to define a comment state:

```
"/*"              {BEGIN(comment);}
<comment>\n       { ++line_num; }
<comment>"*/"     {BEGIN(INITIAL);}
<comment>.        ; // ignore
```

This works, but it is inefficient: every character between /* and */ is processed as a potential match to be returned to Bison. As discussed in the next tip, you usually want to make matches as big as possible, in order to reduce the number of times Flex has to get ready to invoke user code. If we tried to fix this problem by updating the pattern to .*, we would encounter the greedy-match problem again.

However, there is a better solution, one that addresses all of our constraints: calling input() yourself[8]. The following is Flex's recommended solution:

---

[8] Or yyinput if you are generating a C++ scanner.

```
"/*" {
  int last_was_asterisk = 0;
  while (1) {
    int ch = input();
    if (ch == 0⁹) {
      printf("Error: Runaway comment");
      break;
    } else if (last_was_asterisk
        && ch == '/') {
      break;
    } else if (ch == '\n') {
      ++line_num;
    }
    last_was_asterisk = (ch == '*');
  }
}
```

---

9 Some implementations use EOF; that is actually incorrect.
EOF is a C macro defined to be less than zero, but `input()`
returns 0 at the end of all input.

2.2.2 Match the biggest strings possible

The motivation for maximizing the size of Flex's matches is to minimize the number of them, for the cost paid crossing the bridge to Bison is relatively expensive. The Flex manual highly suggests reducing the number of `returns`, especially for cases like parsing block comments. (See previous tip.)

However, you do not want to make the match obnoxiously large. Flex's `yytext` buffer has only a certain size, and if the token exceeds that size, Flex has to reallocate the buffer. This resizing is a very costly operation: not only does it invoke `malloc`, but also it has to rescan the current token (which is, by definition, large). Fortunately, the default size of the buffer is 8kB, which is about three orders of magnitude bigger than the average token.

In practice, this tip is mostly relevant for guiding the solution to scanning block comments; I mention it only in case you find a similar situation in which it applies.

2.2.3 Prefer <<EOF>> over yywrap

<<EOF>> is a special pattern. When Flex encounters the end of a file, it first checks yywrap to see if there are more files to process. If not (i.e. yywrap returns nonzero), then Flex checks for any <<EOF>> rule that applies.

However, you cannot use <<EOF>> as part of a pattern, such as this valiant effort to catch missing close-quotes:

```
"[^"]*<<EOF>>      ; // error
```

Instead, you would have to put <<EOF>> inside of a start-state[10]:

```
"                    {BEGIN(QUOTE_STATE);}
<QUOTE_STATE>"        ;
<QUOTE_STATE><<EOF>>  ; // error
```

Another aspect of <<EOF>> that makes it special is that without a start-state designation, it is a catch-all for *all* start-states that do not have their own <<EOF>> pattern. In other words, every start-state is non-exclusive for the <<EOF>> pattern!

As for yywrap, you must either define it yourself, link in the empty definition with -lfl, or disable it completely. I advocate the latter:

```
%option noyywrap
```

So why prefer <<EOF>> over yywrap? The stated

---

[10] This is not the best way to handle either quoted strings or catching unclosed quotes. See §2.4.4.

purpose of `yywrap` is to enable you to chain input files together, such as for the `cat` program. Consider, though, that an implementation of `cat` using `yywrap` would have both pattern rules and the `yywrap` function; an implementation using <<EOF>> would have only pattern rules. Keeping all the code in one place is a maintenance win.

A better reason to prefer <<EOF>> is that since it is a pattern rule, it is much more obvious what it does. Remember the first time you encountered `yywrap` — did the name immediately tell you what it does?

If your application does chain files together, be sure to call `yyrestart` so that Flex can ensure the buffers are synchronized. A good implementation of <<EOF>> to read multiple files might be:

```
<<EOF>> {
  if (more-files) {
    yyin = fopen(...);
    if (!yyin) ...error...
    yyrestart(yyin);
    BEGIN(INITIAL); // if applicable
  }
  else {
    yyterminate();
  }
}
```

For more information, the end of chapter 9 of the Flex manual covers `yywrap`, and chapter 12 covers <<EOF>>.

2.2.4 Use `yyleng` instead of `strlen(yytext)`

As part of its token packaging at the end of a pattern match, Flex sets the value of `yyleng` to the length of `yytext`. It is the same value as `strlen(yytext)`[11], but calling `strlen` invokes function overhead and performs a linear-time calculation of the string length.

For squeezing out every last cycle of performance, it would be ideal if we could pass `yyleng` to `strdup` in order to prevent its internal call to `strlen`[12]. Instead, we could make our own string-copying function that uses `yyleng` instead of `strlen` (and also uses `yytext` globally instead of pushing it on and off the stack):

```
%{
char* my_strdup();
%}
%%
[a-zA-Z]+   {
    yylval = my_strdup();
    return STRING;
  }
%%
char* my_strdup() {
  char *res = malloc(yyleng + 1);
  strcpy(res, yytext);
  return res;
}
```

---

[11] For non-binary data.

[12] `strndup` copies at most n characters, but does not use n to guide memory allocation.

30

2.3 Robustness

2.3.1 Match all possible input

Ideally, the patterns in each of your Flex states will match all possible inputs. It is easy to match the input you expect, but it is harder to anticipate completely unexpected input.

The default catch-all rule in Flex is simple: it matches any single character, and the action is to print it on stdout:

```
. | \n    ECHO[13]
```

This is a good first step in that at least unhandled input is not swept under the rug, but it is not ideal. By printing out unmatched input, the error (incomplete pattern coverage) manifests as something completely different (occasional random characters on stdout). It is best to promote this from an indirect warning to an actual error. There are two ways we could do that. The first is to promote it from a lexing problem to a parsing problem:

```
. | \n    { return yytext[0]; }
```

The advantage of this is that the error can be put in context, so the message may be more helpful to the end user.

The second method is to make it an explicit Flex error:

---

[13] Do not use a character class here. [.\n] matches carriage returns and a literal period, not all characters.

```
.|\n   {
   fprintf(stderr,
      "ERROR: unhandled input '%s'\n",
      yytext);
   exit(-1);
}
```

The advantage to this method is that you get warnings at compile-time instead of errors at run-time. Flex already issues warnings about pattern coverage, but the implicit ECHO rule silently fills any holes, effectively disabling the warning. You can disable the implicit ECHO rule with the following:

```
%option nodefault
```

While I recommend that option, I do not recommend trying to rely exclusively on Flex's warnings. First, without any catch-all, Flex's warning message is not helpful for indicating the specific problem:

```
warning, -s option given but default
rule can be matched
```

Additionally, it is always a run-time error when any hole is encountered, and the error message is even less helpful:

```
flex scanner jammed
```

2.3.2 Match illegal input

When illegal input happens, it usually throws your lexer and/or parser into a confused state, because it is not entirely sure what is going on. Worse, when a confused parser generates subsequent errors, the messages become progressively less likely to be accurate or helpful. Imagine something as simple as forgetting a closing quote:

```
var = "some value;
some_function(var);
```

If this particular language allowed carriage returns in strings, then it would continue scanning until it found the start of the next string, and generate errors trying to parse its contents. If the language did not allow carriage returns in strings, and you followed the previous tip to implement your own catch-all, then you would get an error saying that the quote character is unhandled input.

Instead, you would really like the error message to indicate the real problem, which is the lack of a closing quote. The best way to do that is with an additional pattern that specifically checks for missing closing quotes. For the case where the language does not allow carriage returns in strings, then you could do something like this[14]:

---

[14] This is not the best way to handle quoted strings, particularly if you have to support escaping. See §2.4.4.

33

```
CHR [^"\n]
%%
\"{CHR}*\"   {
    // Process string
  }
\"{CHR}*   {
    // Issue error about unclosed quote
  }
```

If the language does allow carriage returns in strings, your options are much more limited. The typical approach is to remember whether the most recent string had carriage returns in it, and if so then any subsequent parse error can suggest that the problem might be an unclosed quote. For example, perl's error message is:

```
syntax error at $file line $num, near
"$token" (Might be a runaway multi-line
string starting on line $num)
```

Matching illegal input is a powerful mechanism for making your parser more robust in the face of input errors.

2.3.3 Do not overflow the buffer

Currently, the default size of Flex's token buffer is 16kB (16,384 bytes). Although that is quite large for a token, it is still finite, so it is possible to overflow. Overflowing is not a critical problem (Flex will just upsize the buffer and restart the scan), but it is a time and memory drain you should avoid if you know it is a possibility.

The key element contributing to the length of a token is your own patterns. Far and away the worst problems happen with * and +. We saw this when handling block comments in §2.2.1, but a similar case is handling quoted strings. Like comments, quoted strings suspend the normal handling of language elements (such as keywords and parsing rules) until the closing quote is seen, so you could be lulled into the same initial solution:

```
\"(.|\n)*\"    { ... }
```

This inherits all of the problems mentioned in §2.2.1: it is a greedy match that will initially go past the first close-quote it sees, it does not account for updating line numbers, but most importantly has no size limitation and risks an overflow. Once again you may be tempted to use start-states, but that is still not an optimal solution.

At the very least you can fix the greedy matching problem (and thus lower the probability of overflowing the buffer) by changing (.|\n)* to [^"]*:

```
\"[^"]*\"
```

However this is functionally incorrect if the language allows you to escape quote characters. See §2.4.4

for handling quoted strings most effectively.

A final risky situation for buffer upsizing is when you have enabled . to match \n; but the syntax for doing so is visually distinctive, and at least this situation is less likely to slip past you:

```
(?s:"//".*)   {
        // (Supposed to be comment to
        // end-of-line; accidentally
        // consumes the rest of the input)
    }
```

2.3.4 How to reset correctly

Flex's entry point (`yylex`) is a coroutine, which necessarily means it stores state between invocations. This makes it essential to correctly reset Flex's state between inputs, especially for interactive lexers but even when you read multiple unrelated files. The two important functions are `yylex_destroy` and `yyrestart`.

You should call `yylex_destroy` first, which does the following:
- cleans up and resets the current stack of buffers
- resets Flex's global variables

Part of reseting the global variables includes `yy_start`, so you do not need to call `BEGIN(INITIAL)` as well. However, if you want to start in a specific state, just remember to invoke `BEGIN` after the call to `yylex_destroy`.

When you have the next input file ready to read, set `yyin` and then call `yyrestart`. It sets up Flex's buffer so that subsequent reads come from the new stream.

As for *when* to reset Flex, that should be whenever the input changes without preserving context. For example, in `yywrap`/`<<EOF>>` if you are processing multiple files that do not relate to each other. Another example is after each error in an interactive application.

```
<<EOF>>   {
    yylex_destroy();
    yyin = fopen(...);
    yyrestart(yyin);
}
```

2.4 Functionality

2.4.1 Copy string matches

When Flex finds a match, it returns both a token and a value to Bison for further use in grammar actions. However, string values are (usually) stored in a `char*` variable, and `char*` variables do not copy-by-value the same way that other primitives do. Specifically, when you assign one `char*` variable to another, you merely copy the address of a string from one variable to another; the string itself is not copied. Your "copy" becomes invalid as soon as control leaves the pattern's code block, so you must fully copy string values in some manner.

The easiest and most common approach is to copy it via `strdup`, but that is not your only option. If you are using C++, you can leverage `std::string`, since it copies the `char*` string you build it from. Or you could allocate and copy using `malloc` and `strcpy` yourself, to make your own string-duplication function such as the optimization idea in §2.2.4.

A subsequent common pitfall that bears repeating is that the consumer eventually needs to remember to free string memory.

Here is a minimal example for returning an IDENTIFIER-type token:

```
    // Bison's .y
%union {
  char *sval;
}
%token <sval> IDENTIFIER


    // Flex's .l
[a-zA-Z0-9_]+  {
    yylval.sval = strdup(yytext);
    return IDENTIFIER;
  }
```

2.4.2 Know the limits of regexs

Regular expressions are very powerful, but they cannot express all possible patterns. Their key limitation is the lack of memory: for example, by themselves you cannot match the nesting of opening/closing braces.[15] In fact this applies to all nestable elements, such as parentheses, which implies you cannot use Flex alone to parse mathematical expressions.

Another class of problems that regexes cannot handle is matching counts of elements. For example, any number of zeroes (or any pattern) followed by the same number of ones (or any other pattern)[16]:

```
01
0011
000111
```

Another more general example is merely matching the same number of two different patterns:

```
0011
0101
1010
0110
```

Most humorously, it turns out you cannot use a regex to match a regex[17].

_____

[15] Back-references add substantial power to regular expressions, but Flex does not support them. (And even if it did, it would be quite dodgy to use them in a scanner.)

[16] Though it is easy (and a different problem) if you know the exact number beforehand.

[17] Because of those parentheses.

Less abstractly, Flex's patterns have some
limitations and caveats to be aware of. First and foremost
is that . does not match \n, an intentional decision that
has tripped up many new Flex users.

An actual limitation is that Flex does not support
the shorthand character classes, such as \d meaning
[0-9], \D for [^0-9], or \w for [a-zA-Z0-9_], though
it does (almost) have equivalents:

```
[[:digit:]]
[^[:digit:]]
[[:alnum:]_]
```

Sadly, not only does Flex not have \b (for word
boundaries), it barely has an equivalent. The closest
solution is trailing context, which of course works only at
the end of patterns.

2.4.3 Use `REJECT` to get around some context limitations

Occasionally you encounter a contextual dependency in a language. My pet example is version strings, which could literally be `3.14` and "misparsed" as a number instead of as a string:

```
// Bison grammar:
version_pattern: VERSION STRING .

// Flex patterns:
version          { return VERSION; }
[0-9]+\.[0-9]+   { return NUMBER; }
[a-zA-Z0-9\.]*   { return STRING; }
```

This works on the input `version v3.2` (and even `version 3.2.1`) but fails on `version 3.2`.

One solution is using the `REJECT` macro when we know the first match is not actually the right one. For this to work, we need to be able to distinguish context; for this trivial example we will assume that any `version` in the input is supposed to be followed by a version string:

```
// Flex patterns:
version          {
    expecting_string = true;
    return VERSION;
}
[0-9]+\.[0-9]+   {
    if (expecting_string) REJECT;
    return NUMBER;
}
[a-zA-Z0-9\.]*   {
    expecting_string = false;
    return STRING;
}
```

Note that this endorsement of REJECT contradicts §2.6.1, which says not to use it for speed reasons. If speed is at all a concern, try to find a non-REJECT way to resolve context dependencies.

2.4.4 Handling escape characters

Interpreting escape characters in your input is a little tricky because you need those control characters to not fool the lexer. Or rather, since their whole point *is* to fool the lexer, you need them to fool the lexer in the exact right way. There are two elements to this: identifying escape sequences, and mapping them into their final value. For example, \" would remove the slash, effectively replacing it with just "; \n would be replaced with ASCII 10 (and/or ASCII 13, or something else depending on your platform).

There are several ways for trying to deal with escape sequences. The first three are unusable (regexes, start states, yyless+yymore), but we will still discuss them in case their unusability is enlightening.

The regex method tries to include escapes in normal patterns. A baseline pattern for quoted-strings (before adding support for escapes) might look like this:

```
QUOTE    \"
CHAR     [^\"]
%%
{QUOTE}{CHAR}*{QUOTE}   {
    // Usual quoted string.
  }
```

The first complexity to extending this to allow escaped quotes is that normal characters are a single character but escape sequences are multiple characters. That is, we have to modify CHAR to accept either a single unescaped character or the two-character sequence \", which might look like this:

44

```
SINGLE_CHAR   [^\"\\]
ESCAPE_SEQ    \\\"
CHAR {SINGLE_CHAR}|{ESCAPE_SEQ}
```

Notice that the single-character pattern has to exclude backslashes, because now they have a special meaning.

This solved our immediate problem, but just created another: now we cannot have a backslash as the last character of the string, because it looks like an escaped quote. In fact, any time you introduce escape sequences you have to add the ability to escape the escape sequence. Fortunately this is easy, because we can group all the valid escape sequences in a character class:

```
ESCAPE_SEQ \\[\"\\]
```

However, this pattern will fail on unknown escape sequences such as \4. It is application-dependent how you want to handle this (that is, allow any possible escape sequence vs. let it be an input error propagated back to the user). This pattern will have it manifest as an input error, so let us explore how to be as robust as possible and allow unknown escapes. In that case, the pattern for an escape sequence needs to recognize every possible character after an initial backslash:

```
ESCAPE_SEQ \\(.|\n)
```

Now we can finally move on to mapping the sequences into their corresponding values. Since the escapes are included in yytext, we have to post-process it using string operations to do the conversions - and this presents a few new challenges. First is that there is no simple C function to say, "convert all instances of \n into

45
```
```

ASCII 10", which means you have to do it yourself; second, even if there were such a function, a literal substitution would incorrectly apply to an input such as `foo\\noo`, because the backslash itself is escaped.

Sadly, having come this far, we realize the pattern approach is probably not a great solution here.

A second possible method for handling escape sequences is to use start-states. Specifically, we could have a pattern for each escape sequence, translate it by editing `yytext` directly, and use `yymore` to continue on until the closing quote. This is not a bad thought - start states let us isolate the handling for escape syntax, they continue to rely on Flex to match patterns for us, and we can translate escape sequences as soon as we recognize them. However, there is a crippling problem with this approach — due to how `yymore` works, you cannot edit `yyleng` at the same time[18]. Since that means it will not let us translate two escape characters into one final character, this is a non-starter.

A third method for handling escaped quotes is mentioned in *Flex & Bison* — using `yyless` with `yymore`, and without start-states. The idea is to let an escaped quote incorrectly match, and then manually get it back on track:

---

[18] There is some internal state that does not pick up on changes to `yyleng`.

```
\"[^"]*\" {
  // If the final quote was escaped:
  if (yytext[yyleng-2] == '\\') {
    // Return last quote to input:
    yyless(yyleng-1);
    // Tell it to continue on:
    yymore();
  }
}
```

However, there are some problems here, too. First, this does not perform the translation, so \" is preserved as \", and we have the same post-processing problem we had with the pattern solution. Second, it recognizes only escaped quotes, not arbitrary escape sequences such as \n. Worst of all, though, this does not recognize an escaped escape at the end of the string - an input of "foo\\" will fool it into thinking the closing quote is escaped.

The final method for handling escape sequences is to give up on trying to match it with any number of clever patterns and just use input() to do it yourself. This is rather manual, but it is the only way to have direct control over the recognition and translation of escape sequences. One caveat: this solution requires %array (which is *not* the default), as you cannot add to yytext with %pointer. This solution satisfies all of our constraints:

• It recognizes all escape sequences correctly, including escaped backslashes.

• It translates all escape sequences correctly.

• As a bonus, the initial and final quote characters are trimmed off, saving an additional post-processing step for the consumer.

```
%array
%%
\"   {
  yyleng = 0;   // overwrite quote char
  char ch;
  while ((ch = input()) && ch != 0) {
    // Make sure we do not go past
    // the end of the buffer:
    if (yyleng == YYLMAX); // error
    // Handle an escape:
    else if (ch == '\\') {
      ch = input();
      if (ch == 0); // error
      else if (ch == 'n') {
        // Carriage return
        yytext[yyleng++] = 10;
      }
      else {
        // No special treatment other
        // than to not add the escape
        // character to yytext:
        yytext[yyleng++] = ch;
      }
    }
    // End of string:
    else if (ch == '"') {
      // Overwrite quote char with EOS:
      yytext[yyleng] = 0;
      return STRING;
    }
    // Normal character:
    else {
     yytext[yyleng++] = ch;
    }
  }
```

2.4.5 Handle pattern ties correctly

As far as Flex is concerned, a tie is when two patterns equally match the input. This is quite common; for example, consider the rule for matching the keyword while and the rule for matching identifiers:

```
FIRST_CHAR [a-zA-Z_]
CHAR [a-zA-Z0-9_]
%%
{FIRST_CHAR}{CHAR}*   { // identifier }
while                 { // keyword }
```

Given an input of while (foo), both patterns would accept the initial 5 characters as a match.

Another situation where this ambiguity can occur is numbers and unquoted strings, such as my pet example[19] that declares a version with an unquoted string:

```
VERSION 5.2
```

Since version numbers can theoretically have three fields (5.2.8?), or maybe just one, or maybe any number of fields, a pattern for it would look very similar to the pattern for regular numbers:

```
[0-9]+(\.[0-9]+)*   { // version number }
[0-9]+(\.[0-9]+)?   { // regular number }
```

Flex has two ways to breaks ties. The first is by the length of the match. In our while example, both the identifier pattern and the keyword pattern match 5 characters, so it is still a tie. Even in our version number example, both 123 and 123.456 will match both patterns.

---

[19] DEF (Design Exchange Format), also discussed in §2.4.3.

However, `123.456.789` will match only a version-number, because it is longer than what the regular-number pattern can match.

The second way Flex breaks ties is by choosing the pattern that is listed first in your Flex input. For the `while` example, you would want to list the keyword rules before the identifier rule, to give them precedence:

```
FIRST_CHAR [a-zA-Z_]
CHAR [a-zA-Z0-9_]
%%
while                  { // keyword }
{FIRST_CHAR}{CHAR}*    { // identifier }
```

And in general, you want to list your most specific patterns before the more general ones. Luckily, when you get them backwards, Flex will issue a warning:

```
warning, rule cannot be matched
```

However, neither of these tie breakers satisfactorily resolves the version-number problem. If we listed regular-number pattern first, then a version string of `5.8` would be lexed as a regular-number instead of as a version-number; but if we listed version-number first, then a coordinate of `5.8` would be lexed as a version number! There are several somewhat hacky solutions for this situation. The first is to make the entire version declaration a single token:

```
VERSION[ \t\n]+[0-9]+(\.[0-9]+)*   { .. }
```

To isolate the actual number, you would have to post-process yytext to remove `VERSION[ \t\n]+`. In addition to being messy, this solution assumes nothing is allowed between `VERSION` and the number, which does not apply when the language allows comments.

A better idea is a start-state just for version numbers:

```
%x VERSIONNUM
%%
VERSION    { BEGIN(VERSIONNUM); }
<VERSIONNUM>[0-9]+(\.[0-9]+)* {
    BEGIN(INITIAL);
    // Return yytext as needed
  }
```

(Note that the VERSIONNUM state would have to be %x exclusive if your regular number pattern is not in a state.)

A final idea is to have Bison tell Flex when it should enter that start-state. The above snippet has no context; a VERSION anywhere in the file will trigger the start-state, which may or may not be correct. It is possible for a given lexeme to appear in multiple contexts with completely different meanings (such as - in C, which could be either subtraction or unary negation). Moving the control over to Bison allows you to distinguish context that Flex alone would lack. However, see §3.2.1 for a warning about midrule actions being run after the lookahead token is lexed, which would void this approach with at least this particular example.

2.4.6 Handling multi-start-state patterns

Flex has several start-states mechanisms that allow you to specify that a pattern should apply in multiple states, which is great for reducing copy-paste.

The first mechanism is for matching an explicit list of states:

```
<s1,s2>[0-9]+"."[0-9]+   { ... }
```

This allows this pattern to match in states s1 and s2, but not in any others. Since this list is obvious and explicit, this is a highly maintainable approach. Note that you can include INITIAL in the state list.

The second mechanism is for matching in all states:

```
<*>[0-9]"."[0-9]+   { ... }
```

This applies to all states, including INITIAL. This syntax is also clearly understandable; the only red flag is that any new states you create implicitly pick up these patterns whether you meant them to or not. However, this is still the best way to have a global start-state that applies even in exclusive start-states.

The final mechanism is exclusive vs. non-exclusive states:

```
   // s1 is a non-exclusive state:
%s s1
   // s2 is an exclusive state:
%x s2
...
abc         { ... }
<s1>ab      { ... }
<s2>abcd    { ... }
```

With an input of abcd to this contrived example, you get different matches in each state:

- In no state (i.e. INITIAL), only the first pattern applies.
- In state s1, the first two patterns apply (because s1 is non-exclusive, so patterns without states are considered), and since they both match, Flex breaks the tie by going with the first pattern since its match is longer.
- In state s2, only the third pattern applies (because s2 is exclusive).

Of the three mechanics, this is the most complex, and arguably the hardest to maintain. Not only do maintainers have to be fluent with exclusive vs non-exclusive start-states, but also the code is distributed around the source file, which means it could be not obvious what it is happening. (As you saw in the example, the s1 pattern ab was an actual match, but still not chosen; staring at the pattern to figure out why will not help until you scroll up and see that s1 was declared as non-exclusive.)

As a final note, there is one bit of syntactic sugar available to reduce copy-paste even more: the ability to list patterns in a block that applies to multiple start-states:

```
<s1,s2>{
    abcd    {...}
    efgh    {...}
}
<*>{
    ijkl    {...}
}
```

Note that the syntax is strict: you cannot have whitespace around the commas, nor can you have whitespace between the closing > and the opening {. However, you can indent patterns inside the braces, which you normally cannot do.

2.4.7 Handling #include

C's #include is a mechanism that essentially inlines the contents of a specified file. It has been echoed in many other languages, and handling it correctly requires some attention to detail.

The reason we cover #include in the Flex chapter is because it is a lexer-level construct and not a parser-level construct (that is, a Bison grammar for C would not have a rule for #include). It is possible to have a similar mechanism that does operate at the parser level[20], and that has even more considerations that we will not go into here.

The complexity with #include is saving and restoring all the state necessary to be functionally correct. The input buffer changes to a new file, the line number resets to 1, and the input file name (for inclusion in error messages) changes to a new path, but all of these get restored when the #include'd file is done. Worse, since #include'd files can #include other files, we have to use a stack to keep track of everything through arbitrary nesting.

In the interest of completeness, we are also going to save and restore the Flex start-state here. Strictly speaking, this is not part of C's #include, but I cover it in case you encounter a use case that requires it.

Because the input buffer is cached, it is not correct to merely change yyin to a new input. Fortunately, Flex has YY_BUFFER_STATE objects to help manage buffer state, and there are two ways to use them. The yy_switch_to_buffer function directly switches yyin

---

[20] For example, perl's require

(and other state) from the current buffer to another buffer; the `yypush_buffer_state` and `yypop_buffer_state` functions maintain an internal stack. At first blush, the stack mechanism seems like exactly what we want. However, when we are in `<<EOF>>` and wondering whether we should continue on or `return 0`, our only option is to check `yy_buffer_stack_top` (the index of the top of the buffer stack).[21] As that is a bit clunky, I agree with *Flex & Bison*'s choice to maintain your own stack mechanism. In fact, this tip is largely walking through each element of its Example 2-3.

The buffer element of the stack is straightforward, and we are also going to include a pointer to the file so we can `fclose` it later:

```
struct bufstackstr {
    // This stack is implemented as a
    // linked list:
    struct bufstackstr *prev;
    // YY_BUFFER_STATE is a typedef of a
    // pointer, so no asterisk here:
    YY_BUFFER_STATE buff;
    // Opened FILE object:
    FILE *file;
};
struct bufstackstr *bufstack=0;
```

The initial file opening is handled the same way as opening an include file:

---

[21] It would be nice if `yypop_buffer_state` returned whether we reached the end of the stack.

```
// Open the file:
FILE *myfile = fopen(mypath, "r");
if (!myfile) …error…

// Create a buffer object:
YY_BUFFER_STATE mybuff =
  yy_create_buffer(myfile, YY_BUF_SIZE);
if (!mybuff) …error…

// Push it on to our custom stack:
struct bufstackstr *mystackobj =
  malloc(sizeof(struct bufstackstr));
mystackobj->prev = bufstack;
mystackobj->buff = mybuff;
mystackobj->file = myfile;
bufstack = mystackobj;

// Switch yyin (and other state) to the
// new buffer:
yy_switch_to_buffer(mybuff);
```

Later, when we have finished processing this file, we simply undo all of the above:

```
// Pop it from the custom stack:
struct bufstackstr *popped_bufstack =
  bufstack;
bufstack = bufstack->prev;

// Close the file:
fclose(popped_bufstack->file);

// Delete the buffer:
yy_delete_buffer(popped_bufstack->buff);

// Delete the stack object memory:
free(popped_bufstack);

// Switch buffer:
yy_switch_to_buffer(bufstack->buff);
```

Now that we have the core code for stack manipulation, we realize we have to call the `push` code twice: once for the top level file, and once in our `#include` handler. Thus, it really belongs in its own function. (*Flex & Bison* put it in `newfile`.) The `pop` code, however, will only be called once (from inside <<EOF>>), so I leave it inlined. (*Flex & Bison* put it in `popfile`.)

The first of many problems to address is that the last invocation of the <<EOF>> code will be the end of the stack, and should `return 0` instead of switching to a nonexistent buffer. This is easy to check; just before calling `yy_switch_to_buffer`, see if we have exhausted the stack:

```
// If there is nothing more on the
// stack, then we are done with all
// input:
if (!bufstack) return 0;
```

Next, we upgrade the stack to include the file name and line number. It is easy to add two new fields to `struct bufstackstr`:

```
char *filename;
int linenum;
```

Then we update the push code to store them. In an odd twist, notice that we are storing the *current* line number into the *next* buffer, even though the current line number is an attribute of the *current* file. This is a weird case just because line numbers increment the global `yylineno` variable, instead of `bufstack->linenum`[22].

---

[22] Which would be academically possible, if you are not relying on `%option yylineno` to count for you.

```
// Store current line number:
mystackobj->linenum = yylineno;
// Reset yylineno for the new file:
yylineno = 1;
// Store next file name:
mystackobj->filename = strdup(mypath);
```

Predictably, the inverse code restores `yylineno`, and we need to clean up the memory for the `filename` field:

```
// Restore line number:
yylineno = popped_bufstack->linenum;
// Clean up filename memory:
free(popped_bufstack->filename);
```

As a quick aside, here is how to access this file name and line number inside Flex code blocks (or in a custom `yyerror` function):

```
printf("'%s' found on line %i of %s\n",
  yytext,
  yylineno,
  bufstack->filename);
```

Finally, let's also save and restore the current start-state. Flex includes functions for managing a stack of start-states (`yy_push_state`, `yy_pop_state`), but since we already have our custom stack let's treat it like the others. The addition to `struct bufstackstr` is easy:

```
int startstate;
```

Note that `startstate` is like the `linenum` field - it also records the *current* value in the *next* stack frame, and for the same reason - the real value is in a global variable (`yy_start`).

This code assumes you always want to start in INITIAL; adjust this as necessary for your use case:

```
// Save the current start-state:
mystackobj->startstate = yy_start;

// New files start in INITIAL:
BEGIN(INITIAL);
```

The inverse code is almost predictable, except that we cannot use BEGIN to return to the previous state. (BEGIN is a macro that does math on its argument.) Instead, since we queried yy_start directly, we set it directly:

```
// Restore the start-state:
yy_start = popped_bufstack->startstate;
```

And that is it! A full listing of this code, not all chopped for explanation, is in Appendix B.

A final note: if you are using Bison's locations feature, you will need to save and restore four fields (first_line, first_column, last_line, last_column) instead of just one (linenum).

2.5 Code Conventions

2.5.1 Consider carefully before deciding whether to use character class expressions

Flex's character class expressions are a mixed bag. On the one hand, they are a higher-level description of your intent with no runtime cost. Here are three different ways to specify a pattern for an example identifier token:

```
ident   [a-zA-Z][a-xA-Z0-9]*
ident   [[:alpha:]][[:alpha:][:digit:]]*
ident   [[:alpha:]][[:alnum:]]*
```

Did you catch that the first pattern has a bug in it? For this example, the character classes made it less error-prone.

On the other hand, the character classes create two conventions that Flex developers have to remember: the mappings of all the defined classes, and the ambiguous extra brackets.

The character classes are confusingly named. Is \n part of [:blank:]? What is the distinction between [:blank:] and [:space:]? Why is it named [:space:] if it contains more than just the space character? Why is there an [:xdigit:] for hex numbers, but no [:odigit:] for octals? What is the point of (and distinction between) [:graph:], [:print:], and [:cntrl:]? Despite being a feature meant to improve code readability, readability actually suffers if the next person to read your code is not fluent with the above questions.

Another problem with character classes is their

syntax. Notice in the original example that manually specifying the character ranges was actually *more* succinct than using the classes. Worse, their brackets make it easy to forget you need another pair of brackets; [:lower:] does not mean [a-z], it means a-z![23]

One nifty thing is that character class expressions can be negated with a caret. [:^alnum:] matches any character that is not alphanumeric. This can even be combined with other character classes: [[:digit:] [:^print:]] would match all control characters and all digits.

For completeness, here is the list of the character classes that Flex recognizes:

```
[:lower:]   a-z
[:upper:]   A-Z
[:alpha:]   [:upper:][:lower:]
[:digit:]   0-9
[:xdigit:]  [:digit:]a-fA-F
[:alnum:]   [:alpha:][:digit:]
[:blank:]   \ \t
[:space:]   \t\n\f\v\ \13
[:punct:]   !"#$%&'()*+,-./:;«=»?@[\
\]^_`{|}~
[:graph:]   [:alnum:][:punct:]
[:print:]   \ [:alnum:][:punct:]
[:cntrl:]   [:^print:]
```

----

[23] Most of the time. Character classes only behave inside brackets. [[:lower:]] is literally turned into [a-z], but outside of brackets, [:lower:] is not literally turned into a-z.

2.5.2 Quote patterns only when necessary

Flex patterns can be quoted to indicate that regex characters should not be interpreted as regex characters (though C escape sequences such as \n are still interpreted as usual). Quoting is necessary and useful (and has no impact on performance). However, if it is overused, it is very easy to fall into the trap of thinking that Flex's syntax requires the left column to be quoted. Abuse of quoting in pursuit of the laudable goal of consistency can then turn into a maintainability issue.

Instead, the best choice is to limit quoting to when it is truly necessary. Hopefully, having a mix of quoted and unquoted patterns is enough to help maintainers avoid an overquoting trap:

```
if      { ... }
then    { ... }
else    { ... }
[a-zA-Z][a-zA-Z0-9]*   { ... }
"..."   { ... }  // special ellipses token
"//"    { ... }  // start line comment
```

It is also helpful to remember that quotes can be used in the middle of patterns, making the intent even more obvious. For example, this pattern from the Flex manual for matching a floating-point number:

```
[0-9]+"."[0-9]*
```

2.5.3 Use start-condition scopes

For sufficiently nontrivial languages, the use of start states can easily involve many repeated state names. For example:

```
p1  { ... }
p2  { ... }
p3  { ... }
<STATE1>p4  { ... }
<STATE1>p5  { ... }
<STATE1,STATE2>p6  { ... }
```

As any style guideline will tell you, copy-pasting incurs a maintenance cost. Here we also incur a readability cost, since programmers will have to continually scan the state names to verify the assumption that adjacent patterns are in the same state. Fortunately, Flex has a solution: start-state scoping:

```
p1  { ... }
p2  { ... }
p3  { ... }
<STATE1>{
   p4  { ... }
   p5  { ... }
   p6  { ... }
}
<STATE2>p6  { ... }
```

However, you will notice that p6 just got duplicated in order to apply to both STATE1 and STATE2. This is possibly a *worse* solution, for now we are not copy-pasting just an easy-to-read state name but rather an arbitrary regular expression! Yet, Flex rescues us again, because start-state scopes can be nested. This gives us an ideally minimal solution:

```
p1   { ... }
p2   { ... }
p3   { ... }
<STATE1>{
   p4   { ... }
   p5   { ... }
   <STATE2>{
      p6   { ... }
   }
}
```

2.5.4 Use named patterns

Flex allows you to name patterns, so that you can use them essentially as macros in other pattern definitions. This is a great help for code organization: not only do names allow you to encode intent, but they also help reduce copy-paste errors.

```
NUMBER  [0-9]+
%%
{NUMBER}   { ... }
<STATE>{NUMBER}   { ... }
```

An important warning: if you put any regex modifier (e.g. an asterisk or a plus) on a named pattern, you should always add parentheses. Without them, it becomes ambiguous what the modifier applies to. For example:

```
MYPATTERN abc
%%
{MYPATTERN}*   { ... }
```

One interpretation is that this is equivalent to abc*, and will thus match ab, abc, abcc, abccc, etc.

Another interpretation reads the curly braces as parentheses, so that this is equivalent to (abc)* and will match abc, abcabc, abcabcabc, etc.

Which is the correct interpretation? Both! It turns out classic Lex did the former while Flex does the latter. The best rule of thumb is to make explicit any ambiguous situation (which has the side effect of increasing portability between Lex and Flex).

```
({MYPATTERN})*   { ... }
```

2.5.5 Match all reserved words

With Flex, you have the option of either directly matching reserved words, or matching generic strings and picking out which ones are reserved. The latter approach necessarily performs many string comparisons. Consider:

```
STRING  [a-zA-Z][a-zA-Z0-9]*
%%
{STRING}  {
  if (!strcmp(yytext, "if")) {
    return IF;
  }
  else if (!strcmp(yytext, "for")) {
    return FOR;
  }
  else if (!strcmp(yytext, "while")) {
    return WHILE;
  }
  else {
    return STRING;
  }
}
```

Flex does the initial work of matching the string pattern, but then the user code runs strcmp up to three times on every string match! Worse, identifiers are fairly common and have to go through all N comparisons every time.

One definite upgrade to this approach is to use something smarter than a gauntlet of strcmp's. For example, a common approach is to use a *trie*, which is a tree-type datastructure whose edges each represent one character. Each of your reserved words would trace a path through the trie, character by character. Thus, the depth of a trie is the length of your longest reserved word. This approach has some fantastic implications: first, you compare only one character at a time (instead of a full string); second, the number of comparisons you do is likely to be smaller (usually the length of your longest reserved word is smaller than the total number of reserved words); third, if at any time the trie does not have a next node for the current character, then you already know your current string is not one of your reserved words.

However, if you make each of your reserved words its own pattern, Flex's normal token recognition state machine is doing the same thing:

```
if          { return IF; }
for         { return FOR; }
while       { return WHILE; }
{STRING}    { return STRING; }
```

Compared to the gauntlet of `strcmp`'s, this has at least the same speed benefit as tries (and is possibly even faster, since Flex's implementation is cooked into code).

Additionally, matching reserved words directly like this is easier to read and update.

The one downside is that the Flex pattern tables will be larger, which will make the generated code larger; the familiar software tradeoff between speed and space.

Finally, it should be noted that this approach applies only when your set of keywords is known at compile-time. If you must support keywords added at runtime, then tries become your best choice.

2.5.6 Use `yylineno`, when it makes sense

One common pet peeve with Flex is that it does not track line numbers for you. In fact it does, but you have to explicitly enable it, and you have to hold its hand. The `yylineno` variable is actually always visible, but Flex will only update it if you specify `%option yylineno`. Then, it will be automatically incremented when Flex sees newline characters in the input, which is a great thing because it means you do not have to worry about doing it yourself.

However, since Flex can do so many different things, it is not perfect. `yylineno` is not reset to an initial value between input files, or saved and restored when you switch buffers. (See §2.4.7 for adding it to the buffer state stack.)

There is an even worse caveat to using `yylineno`: in some cases it can cause serious performance degradation. Namely, when long patterns match newlines, Flex has to retrace to make sure it counts them correctly. The following pattern would trigger this problem:

```
[^"]*
```

If you encounter this situation, one solution is to split it into two patterns that cannot cross lines:

```
[^"\n]*
\n
```

Then `yylineno` carries no penalty, though it creates a new burden by having to deal with multiple tokens.

2.5.7 Use `%options` instead of command-line flags

Flex lets you specify control options through either command-line flags or `%option` declarations in the first section of the file. Of the two, it is preferable to use `%option`. First, it encodes the build options along with the rest of the Flex input, so there is no need to bring along a makefile to specify how it gets built. Better, a change to an `%option` will trigger timestamp-based rebuilds, whereas a change to a commandline option usually does not.

See chapter 16 of the Flex manual for the large number of command line options that have corresponding `%options` you can use instead. The most common one is:

```
%option prefix="foo"
```

which replaces `-P`/`--prefix` to set the prefix of the output files and the renamed `yy*` functions.

Another good one is:

```
%option batch
```

which replaces `-B`/`--batch` if you know you will only ever read from files (i.e. non-interactively). Batch mode is mentioned in §2.6.8 when discussing the speed benefit of `%option never-interactive`.

2.6 Speed

See chapter 17 of the Flex manual for much helpful information on speed-tuning your lexer.

2.6.1 Avoid REJECT

REJECT can occasionally be useful, but in general it is best avoided. In order to reject the current match, Flex has to decide what the next best match is, which makes the lexer larger and slower. In fact, using REJECT even *once* slows down *all* matches. Worse, it prevents use of the -Cf and -CF optimization switches.

Unlike other Flex actions, REJECT is a goto statement, which means that actions after a REJECT are *not* executed. This inconsistency can be quite unexpected.

Also, the use of REJECT suppresses warnings about unmatchable rules (i.e. warning, rule cannot be matched). This makes sense, because any pattern might be the next best match after another uses REJECT. Any mechanism that suppresses warnings should be treated with caution.

Finally, REJECT prevents the scanner from upsizing the input buffer.

If you really need this functionality, you might try using yyless(0) instead, but be careful to avoid an infinite loop, such as by changing state (and remember to make it exclusive!):

```
%x FORCE_STRING

%%

[0-9]+"."[0-9]+   {
    // If we should actually interpret
    // this as a string..
    if (…) {
      BEGIN(FORCE_STRING);
      yyless(0);
    }
    else {
      …process number…
    }
  }
<INITIAL,FORCE_STRING>[^ \t\n]+   {
  …process string…
  BEGIN(INITIAL);
}
```

2.6.2 Avoid trailing context

Trailing context allows you to match a pattern only when it is followed by another pattern. For example:

```
foo/bar
```

matches `foo` but only if it is part of `foobar`.

Like REJECT, using *any* trailing context at all will slow down *all* matches, though the penalty is not as bad as REJECT's. However, in the presence of what is called "variable trailing context", the penalty does become as bad as REJECT's. Variable trailing context means both the base and trailing parts of your pattern could be multiple different-sized matches. For example:

```
(a|bc)/(def|ghij)
```

Here, the base part could be either one or two characters, and the trailing part could be either three or four characters. This is so much worse than basic trailing context that it is better to factor out the base part's "or" condition and make it two patterns:

```
a/(def|ghij)
bc/(def|ghij)
```

You might also consider trying unput or yyless before using trailing context. Retooling this example to use unput would look like this:

```
adef   {
    unput('f');
    unput('e');
    unput('d');
}
aghij  {
    unput('j');
    unput('i');
    unput('h');
    unput('g');
}
bcdef  {
    unput('f');
    unput('e');
    unput('d');
}
bcghij  {
    unput('j');
    unput('i');
    unput('h');
    unput('g');
}
```

The version using yyless is much more compact:

```
adef   {
    yyless(1);
}
aghij  {
    yyless(1);
}
bcdef  {
    yyless(2);
}
bcghij  {
    yyless(2);
}
```

2.6.3 Use `%pointer`

`%pointer` and `%array` specify how Flex should define yytext – as `char*` or as `char[]`. Though `%pointer` is the default, several previous tips require the use of `%array`, such as §2.4.4 (handling escape sequences). In general, you need `%array` if you manipulate yytext, or if you need yytext to remain unmangled after calling `input` or `unput`.

However, `%array` is measurably slower than `%pointer`. If you have no need for `%array`'s functionality, your scanner will be faster with the default of `%pointer`.

2.6.4 Use `yyterminate` if you know you are at end-of-input

`yyterminate` lets you manually declare that Flex has reached the end of the input, even though there is still data to read.

Flex already calls `yyterminate` when it encounters the real EOF, but there are situations where you can save the runtime of further lexing by halting early. One example may be if your application does something similar to `grep -q`, which checks to see if a specific pattern is in the input; once you have found a match, you can `yyterminate` immediately to avoid redundantly processing the remainder of the input.

Another example might be if your language includes a marker for the end of content, to explicitly say the rest of the file should be ignored. Perl has this with `__DATA__`, which semantically means the rest of the file is no longer code but rather text that would be returned by reading from a special file handle.

Finally, you may want to halt after encountering a certain number of errors. In these cases, calling `yyterminate` when you hit the limit is more elegant than calling `exit` or `abort` inside your error function. Note, however, that `yyterminate` does not invoke any code in `<<EOF>>` blocks, so be careful if you have buffer stacks.

2.6.5 Turn on performance options

The two speed considerations that are exposed as command line controls to developers are:

- the degree to which the scanner tables are compressed, and
- the use of `stdio`.

Compressing tables reduces the generated code size, but it means that Flex has to resolve transitions at runtime. ("Compress" is not meant literally; this operation detects when different states have similar transitions and tries to reuse them.)

The main control option is -C, which controls the degree to which tables should be compressed. Its argument is a string of single-character controls:

-Ce: compresses tables and constructs equivalence classes, which incur a slight performance penalty in order to increase table compression. Optimizes compile-time over run-time.

-Cm: compresses tables and constructs meta-equivalence classes, which similarly incur a runtime cost but reduce tables further.

-C: compresses tables but does not construct either equivalence classes or meta-equivalence classes.

-Cf: does not compress tables at all, trading off compile-time to gain run-time.

-CF: does not compress tables, and uses alternate fast scanner tables, which also trades off compile-time to gain run-time but works better in some situations (such as when you match all identifiers and pick out keywords yourself).

-Cr: bypasses stdio, calling the system `read` function instead of either `fread` or `getc`. Do not use this if you read from `yyin` yourself before invoking `yylex`, because the buffers would be out of sync.

-Ca: memory-aligns the table to word boundaries, which will dramatically increase its memory footprint but improve runtime.

Many of -C's options can be combined. For example, -Cem compresses tables, generates equivalence classes, and generates meta-equivalence classes, giving you the smallest possible memory footprint but the worst runtime. -Cfa does not compress tables, and memory-aligns them to word boundaries, giving you the worst memory footprint but one of the best runtimes.

Flex has two options that are aliases to -C configurations. -f is equivalent to -Cfr, which does not compress tables, and bypasses stdio in favor of direct system calls to read. -F is equivalent to -CFr, which is very similar except it uses the alternate fast-scanner tables.

The absolute best performance is likely to come from either -Cfar or -CFar, which bloats the generated code size and memory footprint but enables every optimization. Of these, -Cfar aligns with §2.5.5, which advises you to match your reserved words. However, if the memory footprint from -Ca is too high, -Cfr/-f is also a fine choice.

As a final note, %option full is equivalent to -f, and %option fast is equivalent to -F.

For more discussion on the tradeoffs of these options, see section 16.4 ("Options for Scanner Speed and Size") in the Flex manual.

2.6.6 Turn on performance warnings

Flex is aware of several situations that cause performance issues, so its -p switch will generate warnings about major issues. Specifying it twice (e.g. -p -p) will also warn about minor issues.

There is only a handful of situations it checks for, but it is not a bad idea to look for them all the time. The situations considered major problems are:
- any use of REJECT (see §2.6.1)
- any use of variable trailing context (see §2.6.2)

The following are considered minor problems:
- any use of yymore
- enabling interactive input, which is the default (see §2.6.8)
- the ^ operator (as applied to whole patterns, not inside character grouping brackets).

%option perf-report is equivalent to -p, and literally specifying it twice is equivalent to -p -p.

This quick example shows you the range of messages you can see:

```
%option perf-report
%option perf-report

%%

^foo|bar {
  REJECT;
}
```

Generates these messages on stderr:

79

    tmp.1:21: '^' operator results in sub-
optimal performance
    -I (interactive) entails a minor
performance penalty
    REJECT entails a large performance
penalty

2.6.7 Detect and avoid backtracking

REJECT is not the only situation where Flex has to back up. Consider these two similar rules:

```
foo      {  ...  }
foobar   {  ...  }
```

With an input of foobat, the lexer gets as far as fooba before discovering it does not match the second rule and backs up to accept the first.

The good news is that you can avoid such backup by making sure all the intermediate patterns match something. One approach is to explicitly list all the partial matches:

```
f       {  ...  }
fo      {  ...  }
foob    {  ...  }
fooba   {  ...  }
```

(Presumably foo and foobar are keywords and you would return f, fo, foob, and fooba as generic identifiers.)

Luckily, you do not have to play guess-and-check while visually inspecting your patterns to figure out where Flex is backtracking. The -b command-line switch will tell you every instance of backtracking needed to handle your patterns. It silently generates a side file named lex.backup (or lex.bck on some systems). For the foo/foobar example above, here is the first warning it generates:

```
State #6 is non-accepting -
 associated rule line numbers:
        10        11
 out-transitions: [ o ]
 jam-transitions: EOF [ \000-n  p-\377 ]
```

Since it lists two line numbers[24], this warning applies to both the foo and foobar rules. The out-transition of o means it is warning about anything that is not o; specifically, something like fom. Adding a rule for fo eliminates this warning.

The next warning is for only the foobar rule:

```
State #8 is non-accepting -
 associated rule line numbers:
   12
 out-transitions: [ a ]
 jam-transitions: EOF [ \000-`  b-\377 ]
```

Adding a foob rule eliminates this one, and similarly, adding a fooba rule eliminates the last warning.

You may be wondering why we did not get a warning for the first o. That is, an input of fp would have to backup since it did not match, so we would after to define a rule for just f to resolve it. However, recall that Flex has a default rule to match a single character and echo it to stdout, so that case was already covered.

A much less manual approach to matching all the intermediate patterns is to include a pattern that generally matches everything. It is likely you have a rule for

---

[24] For at least my example, the reported line numbers were off by one — my input had foo on line 9 and foobar on line 10, but the "associated rule line numbers" reports lines 10 and 11.

matching identifiers, and that may already be enough to resolve all of your backtracking. For example, this alone is enough to resolve all of the foo/foobar backups:

```
[a-z]+   { ... }
```

A final note: to see the full performance benefit of avoiding backup, you have to eliminate *all* sources of backup. The last warning generated by our example is this:

```
Compressed tables always back up.
```

To resolve this, you need either the -Cf or -CF switch (which you may already have for performance reasons anyway).

When all backups have been eliminated, the lex.backup file contains just one line:

```
No backing up.
```

You might consider adding grep -q 'No backing up' lex.backup to your build so that it will automatically alert you when a change introduces backup.

2.6.8 Use `%option never-interactive` (or even `%option always-interactive`)

Flex behaves differently with interactive versus batch input. With interactive input, Flex cannot buffer extra characters because it has to react to user input right away[25]; with batch input, Flex assumes it can always read ahead a bit, which ends up being a little faster. A second concern is that to figure out whether a new input source is interactive or batch, Flex calls `isatty()`, which has some additional performance implications.

The first tip is to use `%option never-interactive` if you know for sure that your input will only come from files and never from interactive input. This both avoids the call to `isatty()` and allows Flex to always prefetch the next character.

However, if you know your input will be interactive, you can still at least avoid the call to `isatty()` with `%option always-interactive`. If you have a mix of interactive and batch input, I suggest trying both with and without this on your actual input to quantify which one works better for your application.

There are two other options (`%option batch` and `%option interactive`) which control only whether to prefetch the next character. `%option batch` is redundant because it is implicitly enabled in a few situations:
- with `%option never-interactive`
- when run with `-Cf` or `-CF`.

---

[25] The specific issue is returning tokens as soon as a carriage return is pressed. Normally it would also try to prefetch the next character after it, which may just block the program indefinitely!

Similarly, `%option interactive` (which is the default) is a subset of `%option always-interactive`.

2.7 Gotchas

2.7.1 Be careful with the regex modifiers

Flex lets you use some of the extended regex modifiers, specifically:
- i: make the pattern case insensitive.
- s: forces . (period) to also match \n.
- x: ignores whitespace in the pattern, unless it is escaped, quoted, or in a character class.

(Users of perl will recognize these; *Perl Best Practices*[26] recommends the s and x modifiers on all matches.)

The syntax to use these modifiers is to enclose a pattern in a special (?:...) group with some selection of modifiers. This can make patterns more readable, but it is also pretty likely that most people will not know what they are right away. Usually, general unfamiliarity would be a deterrent for a feature's use, but this syntax is distinct enough that any reasonable user will figure out this is something special. Some specific examples:

```
// Equivalent "i" example:
(?i:ab)     { … }
([aA][bB])  { … }

// Equivalent "s" example:
(?s:c.d)    { … }
(c(.|\n)d)    { … }

// Equivalent "x" example:
(?x:e  f)   { … }
(ef)        { … }
```

---

[26] Damian Conway; 2009

You can include multiple modifiers in a single pattern group:

```
(?ix:g H)   { ... }
```

And, like any other pattern atom, they can be included inside a larger pattern:

```
foo(?s:.)*bar
```

If your keywords are case-insensitive (e.g. COBOL (mostly)), the case-insensitivity modifier is particularly helpful. Consider the two ways to implement it:

```
[kK][eE][yY][wW][oO][rR][dD]  { ... }
(?i:keyword)   { ... }
```

There is no question the second version is both easier to read and less error-prone. (For completeness, Flex can turn on global case insensitivity with %option case-insensitive[27]. Once enabled, however, the only way to reenable case-sensitivity is (?-i:...), and patterns with that need to be listed before the case-insensitive patterns.)

Curiously, case-insensitive identifiers do not benefit as dramatically as keywords did from this modifier:

```
[a-zA-Z][a-zA-Z0-9]*  { ... }
(?i:[a-z][a-z0-9]*)   { ... }
```

We save merely one character, but it does read more easily and is less error-prone.

---

[27] Also usable as %option caseless

87

The s modifier enables . to match \n, which it usually (and specifically!) does not. I recommend against using s at all. First, it does it not save much space; the overhead of (?s:.) is only less than (.|\n) if the pattern has more than one . you want to modify. The more important objection is that if you *want* . to match \n, it is preferable to make it glaringly obvious in the pattern because then the intent is conveyed. Once the eye gets used to the modifier syntax, it can glaze over the semantics of s far more easily than it glazes over an explicit pattern with (.|\n).

The x modifier ignores whitespace in patterns, allowing you to inject spaces for readability. This is especially useful because it allows carriage returns. Consider inheriting a regex for parsing one possible interpretation of floating-point numbers:

```
[-+]?([0-9]+\.?[0-9]*|\.[0-9]+)(e-?
[0-9]+)?   { ... }
```

versus:

```
(?x:
  [-+]?
  (
      [0-9]+\.?[0-9]*
    |
      \.[0-9]+
  )
  ( e -? [0-9]+ )?
)  { ... }
```

It is much easier to read the intent in the second case, which makes it much easier to update later.

2.7.2 $ does not match <<EOF>>

$ is the same as a trailing context of \n (that is, foo$ is the same as foo/\n). However, if the last line of your input is well-formed but does not include a \n, then this pattern does not match, and you get a rather confusing lexing error. It seems obvious, but as an example, consider a file format where each line is expected to be a single word; this syntax is so simple we could check for syntax errors directly in Flex without relying on Bison:

```
^[a-zA-Z]+$   { ... }
.*   { ...unexpected input... }
```

This fails if the last line is missing the carriage return, even though the rest of the line may be okay[28].

Unfortunately, we cannot do something as easy as ending the pattern with ($|<<EOF>>), since <<EOF>> can only be used as a standalone pattern. We have to look for the pattern in three different contexts, in a specific order:

1. at the end of a line (where $ will work)
2. where there is nothing after it (which will be triggered by the EOF)
3. where there *is* something after it (which is what is left over after not matching [1] and [2])

To reuse the above example, we might end up with something like the following:

---

[28] I discovered this particular situation when a co-worker edited an existing file using emacs, which is apparently happy creating a line at the end of the file that ends with EOF instead of a carriage return. To my knowledge, all other editors inject the implied carriage return for you.

```
WORD   [a-zA-Z]+
%%
^{WORD}$    { ...matches at EOL... }
^{WORD}     { ...matches at EOF... }
^{WORD}/.   { ...error... }
```

I reduced pattern duplication by naming the
pattern, but we can also reduce code duplication by using
the special value | as the action for the first pattern, so that
it will use the action from the second pattern:

```
WORD   [a-zA-Z]+
%%
^{WORD}$    |
^{WORD}     { ...matches at EOL or EOF... }
^{WORD}/.   { ...error... }
```

This solution is almost as good as if we were able to
use ($|<<EOF>>)!

2.7.3 Use `unput` sparingly

The `unput` function conceptually pushes input characters back into the input stream, so that they will be the next ones Flex reads. It is occasionally very useful (*Flex & Bison* has an example using it to expand C macros; see page 137), but there are some caveats to be aware of.

First, using `unput` may require `%array`. (Not always; with `%pointer`, both `yytext` and `yyleng` are trashed by `unput`, but that may be okay depending on the application.) §2.6.3 covered why we usually want `%pointer` for performance reasons. If you need `%pointer`, `unput`, *and* the contents of `yytext`, just be sure to copy `yytext` before calling `unput`.

More important, there is a limit to how many characters you can `unput` before it becomes unhappy. Currently, when the `yytext` buffer is full, `unput` will not resize it but rather generate a fatal runtime error. In practice, this is usually a pretty high limit — the `yytext` buffer size (`YY_BUF_SIZE`'s default is at least 16kB) minus what is already in it (`yyleng`).

A final limitation of `unput` is that you cannot use it on `<<EOF>>`. If you are trying to stop processing a file early, `yyterminate` might be more helpful[29].

---

[29] As noted in §2.6.4, though, if you have a stack of buffers, `yyterminate` will not unroll it for you.

2.7.4 Use serialized tables if memory is a concern

Normally, Flex generates huge C arrays to store the transition tables of its core lexing state machine. However, after you have loaded your input, those tables really do not need those to be in memory anymore. Flex's "serialized table" mechanism lets you load and unload the tables on the fly.

The first step is to specify `%options tables-file`, which tells Flex to write the state transitions to that file instead of as usual code output:

```
%option tables-file="my.tables"
```

Next we need to load the tables, which must come before calling `yylex` (and thus `yyparse`):

```
FILE *f_table = fopen("my.tables", "r");
if (!f_table) { ...error... }
if (yytables_fload(f_table)) { ...error... }
```

Finally, when we are done processing all input that needs these tables, we can free the memory they consume:

```
yytables_destroy();
```

Note that the tables files are binary, so you not will be able to peek at them for any interesting information[30].

Also note that while these functions work in reentrant parsers, they are not thread-safe.

---

[30] Chapter 22 of the Flex manual has the file format if you are truly curious.

2.7.5 Initial whitespace is significant

In the first and second sections of the Flex input file, Flex has a nifty "feature" to treat any line with initial whitespace as code to be copied verbatim to the output. This is great for injecting comments in your Flex specification without requiring extra %{...%} blocks, but less nifty if the line is not actually code. Specifically, all of your % declarations in the first section and your pattern definitions in the second section must be left-aligned, and your comments must not be:

```
    // Disable yywrap so that we do not
    // have to link libfl.so
%option noyywrap

%%

    // Consume whitespace
[ \t]+  ;
```

2.8 Development & Debugging

2.8.1 Use `YY_USER_ACTION`, `YY_BREAK`, and/or `-d` to print out matched tokens

An initial approach to printing out all of Flex's matched tokens might be to insert a `printf` statement into every pattern's user code. However, that is either an awful lot of statements to comment out for production, or an awful lot of statements to hide behind `#define` macros.

An alternative, lower-impact solution is to use the `YY_USER_ACTION` macro — Flex inserts an invocation of this macro between the match of each token and its user code, so you merely need to `#define` it as a `printf`. (There is no `%option` for this.)

```
%{
#define YY_USER_ACTION \
    printf("token: '%s'\n", yytext);
%}
```

Additionally, to show which start-state Flex is currently in, you can print `YY_START`. Unfortunately, start states are internally stored only as numbers, so you cannot print out the name of the start state. If it helps, a start-state's number is the order in which it appears in `%s` or `%x` statements.

```
%{
#define YY_USER_ACTION \
    printf("token: '%s', state: %i\n", \
    yytext, \
    YY_START);
%}
```

Finally, if you want to print these messages at the end (instead of beginning) of every block of user code, you can re-#define YY_BREAK instead. The YY_BREAK macro defaults to a single break statement, but you can redefine it to include a print statement. Be extremely careful that your redefinition still ends with a call to break!

```
%{
#define YY_BREAK { \
    printf("token: '%s', state: %i\n", \
        yytext, \
        YY_START); \
    break; }
%}
```

The one downside to these nifty shortcuts is that they do not say *which* pattern matched. That is, it will tell you that "314" is the next token, but not whether it matched it as an integer, a floating-point number, or as a string. We can include the C preprocessor macro __LINE__ to report which line the printf statement happens to land on, which gets us pretty close:

```
%{
#define YY_BREAK { \
    printf("token: '%s', state: %i,
line: %i\n", \
        yytext, \
        YY_START, \
        __LINE__ - 1); \
    break; }
%}
```

However, this trick works only on YY_BREAK, not on YY_USER_ACTION, because YY_USER_ACTION is invoked *before* the generated Flex C code calls #line to adjust line numbers in terms of the Flex input file. Also, since YY_BREAK is always on the next line after the user code, we subtract 1 from __LINE__; this means it reports the last line of the user code for that pattern, not necessarily the line where the pattern definition starts.[31]

Finally, we could run Flex with -d (debug mode), which will print token matches, but also includes the correct starting line number for the pattern:

```
--accepting rule at line 24 ("foo")
```

This is much nicer, though it does not include start-state information. Debug mode also alerts you when the scanner has to back up or accept the default rule, which can be helpful information.

Flex provides a runtime switch (yy_flex_debug) to turn off -d's printfs. This allows you to compile a production scanner with debugging enabled, and then set the switch to 0 so that users do not incur any of the messages in the field...until you want to enable them for debugging.

---

[31] I should mention yy_rule_linenum[yyact] for completeness, which is how Flex itself reports rule line numbers. While yyact is mentioned in the documentation, yy_rule_linenum is not, and I am reluctant to point you to a solution that requires reverse-engineering a generated scanner to discover how to use internal variables correctly. Also, yy_rule_linenum is only visible when the scanner is built in debug mode (-d).

2.8.2 Profiling pattern match hit rate

If you want to count the number of times each pattern is matched, you can use the YY_USER_ACTION macro and the yy_act variable (which is the index of the rule that was matched). With these, you can update an array of hit counts and print it out at the end of your run.

Section 13 of the Flex documentation has a specific example for how to do this; however, the current incarnation has an off-by-one error because yy_act starts counting rule indexes at 1 instead of 0. Here is a modified version:

```
%{
int ctr[YY_NUM_RULES];
#define YY_USER_ACTION { \
    ++ctr[yy_act-1]; \
}
%}
...
int main() {
  ...
  for (int i = 0;
      i < YY_NUM_RULES;
      ++i) {
    ctr[i] = 0;
  }
  ...invoke yyparse/yylex...
  for (int i = 0;
      i < YY_NUM_RULES;
      ++i) {
    printf("  Rule %i: %i\n",
        i+1,
        ctr[i]);
  }
}
```

The size and iteration of ctr should be either

`YY_NUM_RULES` elements (if you have Flex generate a default rule) or `YY_NUM_RULES-1` elements (if you specify `%option nodefault`).

Chapter 3: Bison

Lex & Yacc alleges that you could probably write a specialized, grammar-specific parser that would beat Bison for speed. However, consider the elements of writing your own parser:

- connecting to (and influencing) Flex's token stream
- writing and testing your parser
- implementing your own runtime error recovery

This wheel has already been invented (and debugged!). Even though old software is old, it is also mature – you are almost certain to never encounter a showstopper bug in Bison.

There are some situations where Bison's limitations hold you back. For instance, it is usually limited to one token of lookahead, it does not handle right-recursion well, and getting contextual information to Flex is occasionally problematic. However, there are usually tricks to get around most limitations. If nothing else, ask the Bison mailing list for help – it has plenty of smart people well-versed in practical Bison usage[32].

---

[32] Though they are not going to do your homework for you.

3.1 Core Bison Skills

3.1.1 Understanding rule and reduction values

The ability to associate values with each rule in a Bison grammar (and each token returned by Flex) allows you to manage your program's data flow in a more elegant manner than resorting to more global variables. A common example is a math expression. Consider the following code fragments to implement a trivial addition and subtraction evaluator:

```
// Flex patterns:
[0-9]+   {
    yylval = atoi(yytext);
    return NUMBER;
}
"+"        { return '+'; }
"-"        { return '-'; }

// Bison rules:
%define api.value.type {int}
%token NUMBER
%left '+' '-'
%%
top:
  expr { printf("Result: %d\n", $1); }
  ;
expr: NUMBER           { $$ = $1; }
  | expr '+' expr     { $$ = $1 + $3; }
  | expr '-' expr     { $$ = $1 - $3; }
  ;
```

Flex identifies three tokens (integer numbers, plus signs, and minus signs). The integers have an associated value (the atoi'd version of yytext), while the plus and minus operators do not. Since we defined api.value.type as an int, Bison considers the values for all the non-terminal rules (top and expr) to be ints as well. Thus our blocks of user code can do math operations very easily, and we can elegantly print out the value of the final expression at the end.

For any nontrivial application, token values would not be all the same type. Suppose we wanted to build a syntax tree of the above example instead of directly evaluating it. We might have one object to represent an integer constant, and another object to represent an expression. NUMBER will stay as an int, but now top and expr will be of custom type EFBExpression[33]:

```
%union {
   int int_val;
   struct EFBExpression *expr_val;
}
%token<int_val> NUMBER
%type<expr_val> top
%type<expr_val> expr
%left '+' '-'
```

Correspondingly, our Flex rule for matching integers can no longer assign yylval directly, but now has to specify its int_val field:

```
[0-9]+  {
    yylval.int_val = atoi(yytext);
    return NUMBER;
  }
```

Now we only need to update our Bison rules to create EFBExpression objects. In the interest of brevity I will list possible example code only for addition:

---

[33] "EFB" is for "Effective Flex & Bison"...I'm so creative!

```
%{
struct EFBExpression;
…
struct EFBAddition {
  struct EFBExpression *left;
  struct EFBExpression *right;
};
…
struct EFBExpression {
  union {
    struct EFBAddition    *add;
    struct EFBSubtraction *sub;
    struct EFBConstant    *constant;
  };
  int type;  // 0=add, 1=sub, 2=constant
};

void printEFBExpression(struct
EFBExpression *s) {
  …
}

%}
%%

top:
  expr { printEFBExpression($1); }
  ;

expr: NUMBER { … }
  | expr '+' expr   {
    $$ = malloc(sizeof(struct
EFBExpression));
    $$->type = 0;
    $$->add = malloc(sizeof(struct
EFBAddition));
    $$->add->left = $1;
    $$->add->right = $3;
  }
  | …
```

Here, the reduction of the `expr` rule creates an `EFBExpression` object, and they cascade up as we build the syntax tree.

Presumably, `printEFBExpression` is a recursive function that accounts for the `type` field and handles the expression's payload appropriately.

3.1.2 Understanding precedence and associativity

Precedence and associativity are mechanisms for resolving some ambiguous situations. Provided future maintainers of your code are fluent enough with the ideas, they provide some very elegant solutions.

Math has a long history of precedence and associativity rules, which makes it a great example. Suppose you want to parse the following simple expressions:

```
1 + 2 * 3
4 * 5 + 6
```

Flex reports tokens in left-to-right order, and if Bison reduced rules as soon as it could, you would end up with (1 + 2) * 3 and (4 * 5) + 6. Only the second one is the correct interpretation, and only by luck.

Using Bison's mechanism to specify that * has a higher precedence than + interprets both expressions perfectly. Let's take a closer look at how this works, because math is not the only situation where precedence can be helpful.

The crucial point is when Bison has seen the first three symbols (1, +, 2) and identifies the lookahead (*). At this point it could either reduce the addition, or shift to follow through with the multiplication. Bison compares the precedence you set for the lookahead symbol (*) with the precedence you set for the rule; since * is higher, Bison chooses to shift so that it can handle the multiplication first. In the second expression, Bison sees the precedence of + being lower than the rule's, and thus reduces to handle the multiplication first.

Associativity applies when the precedence of the rule and the token are the same. For example:

```
1 - 2 + 3
```

Even though - and + have the same precedence, `(1 - 2) + 3` is not the same as `1 - (2 + 3)`. Further, unlike the problem with multiplication vs addition, we cannot resolve this ambiguity by giving - higher precedence than +, because this problem merely recurs when you chain subtractions:

```
1 - 2 - 3
```

Again, `(1 - 2) - 3` is not the same as `1 - (2 - 3)`. Associativity gives us the deterministic mechanism for establishing the correct parse tree when the precedences are the same. Almost all math expressions are left-associative. That is,

```
expr OP expr OP expr
```

should be interpreted as `(expr OP expr) OP expr`. Additionally, chained function calls are also left-associative:

```
obj->func1()->func2()
```

should be interpreted as `(obj->func1())->func2()`.

However, chained assignments are right-associative:

```
a = b = c
```

should be interpreted as a = (b = c).

Interestingly, depending on the language, the ternary operator could be either left- or right-associative:

```
a ? b : c ? d : e
```

PHP defines it with left associativity (yielding (a ? b : c) ? d : e), whereas C[34] defines it with right-associativity (yielding a ? b : (c ? d : e)).

Also worth mentioning is %nonassoc, which prevents operators from chaining; Bison will throw an error if it is found in the input. A common example of non-associativity is all the logic operators (less-than, is-equal, etc). Even though the following can make sense to humans:

```
if (foo < bar < bas) ...
```

It would be a nightmare to design a parser to correctly interpret it as "if foo < bar and bar < bas"[35]. However, the above is still legal C, since foo < bar evaluates to an int , and "[inttype] < bas" is perfectly fine. Since it does not do what you expect, declaring < as non-associative would have been a more effective choice, so that the error is caught at compile-time.

Just to review syntax, the following are the relevant Bison symbol declarators:

---

[34] And pretty much everyone else.

[35] bar appears once in the input but would be used twice in the syntax tree!

- `%token`, which does not declare any precedence or associativity.
- `%precedence`, which defines precedence but not associativity
- `%left`, `%right`, and `%nonassoc`, which define both precedence and associativity.

Symbols declared later have higher precedence. That is, be sure to list your declarations in order of increasing priority. All of these declarations allow you to list multiple symbols at a time, which semantically means they all have the same level of precedence. Thus, the correct way to declare math operators would be:

```
%left '+' '-'
%left '*' '/'
```

A rule's precedence is either inherited from the precedence of its final terminal symbol, or explicitly defined with the `%prec` declaration:

```
expr: expr '+' expr %prec '+'
```

Here, `%prec` is redundant because the `'+'` is already the final terminal symbol in the rule.

3.1.3 Understanding shift/reduce conflicts

Suppose you have the following rule:

```
myrule: A
  | A B
  ;
```

After seeing A, Bison could reduce to match `myrule: A`; however, if the lookahead token is B, then it could also shift and then reduce to match `myrule: A B`. This is the essence of shift/reduce conflicts. A common example is the typical `if` statement:

```
if_stmt:
    IF expr THEN stmt
  | IF expr THEN stmt ELSE stmt
  ;
```

After seeing the first `stmt`, Bison could reduce; but if the lookahead token is `ELSE` then it could shift instead. This situation is not too bad; since `ELSE` is not a standalone statement, shifting is the only valid parse. However, a real problem emerges when the first `stmt` is itself another `if_stmt`, giving you the infamous "dangling else" problem:

```
    if cond1 then if cond2 then stmt1 else
stmt2
```

Does the `else` belong with `if cond1` or with `if cond2`? It is ambiguous! Indenting shows you how it could be interpreted either way:

```
// Interpretation 1:
if cond1 then
  if cond2 then
    stmt1
  else  // if !cond2
    stmt2

// Interpretation 2:
if cond1 then
  if cond2 then
    stmt1
else  // if !cond1
  stmt2
```

Of the two, the first interpretation is correct. (To be pedantic, the second interpretation has several problems. First, if another else were added afterward, it would *change the association* of the first else, which presents an obvious readability problem for this language. Second, this amounts to always selecting a reduce in a shift/reduce conflict. To prevent that from issuing a false syntax error on a second else, the parser would have to *count* the final number of else's in a chain before starting any reductions, which means the resolution to a shift/reduce conflict is not to either shift or reduce but rather wait-and-see.)

Bison's default action in shift/reduce conflicts is to shift, which is the first interpretation above. However, Bison will still warn you that there is a shift/reduce conflict, just in case it was not the right thing to do.

Having identified a shift/reduce conflict, how do you fix it? The two basic strategies are to avoid the ambiguity, and to tell Bison explicitly what to do.

To avoid the ambiguity, rearrange the grammar so

that there is only one possible interpretation. This is easier in some cases than in others. The "dangling else" is a notoriously hard case, but one solution would be to introduce an ending token to indicate that the if statement is done. This removes ambiguity by stating that a subsequent else is not part of the current rule:

```
if_stmt:
    IF expr THEN stmt END
    | IF expr THEN stmt ELSE stmt END
    ;
```

After reading IF expr THEN stmt, the next token will be either END or ELSE, so there is no ambiguity about what to do.

As we saw in the previous tip, math is riddled with shift/reduce conflicts, which we resolved with precedence and associativity. My favorite example from *Flex & Bison* was the sneaky way Levine resolved those conflicts with only regular grammar rules and no precedence or associativity:

```
expr:
    factor
    | expr '+' factor
    ;

factor:
    number
    | factor '*' number
    ;
```

The second strategy for resolving shift/reduce conflicts is telling Bison explicitly what to do. This is done by declaring precedence and associativity for tokens and rules. If the next token has a higher precedence than the current rule, then Bison will choose to shift. Thus, we could resolve our dangling-else problem by declaring ELSE with a higher precedence than IF or THEN:

```
%left IF THEN
%left ELSE
```

Another possibility is to declare these tokens as right-associative, which also has the effect of telling Bison to shift instead of reduce:

```
%right IF THEN ELSE
```

An important caveat of using precedence or associativity on non-operator tokens is that Bison will then compare their precedence to actual operators. Consider python's ternary operator:

```
a = b if c else d + 1
```

Is else meant to have lower precedence than +, yielding this:

```
a = b if c else (d + 1)
```

Or is else meant to have higher precedence, yielding this:

```
a = (b if c else d) + 1
```

Worse, having resolved this shift/reduce conflict by explicitly declaring precedence/associativity, Bison will no longer issue warnings about it.[36]

---

[36] Remember to add -v to your Bison runline so that it will create the .output file with the conflict report.

3.1.4 Understanding reduce/reduce conflicts

A reduce/reduce conflict occurs when two rules reduce the same sequence of tokens. Reduce/reduce conflicts are more serious than shift/reduce conflicts, and usually indicate something very bad in the grammar. Here is the essence of reduce/reduce conflict:

```
foo: A B C ;
bar: A B C ;
```

A common practical situation is where the input is empty:

```
optional_list:
  %empty
  | optional_list optional_item
  ;

optional_item:
  %empty
  | item
  ;
```

Is an input of nothing an empty `optional_item` or an empty `optional_list`? The answer matters because it affects the value of the final token, and which user code blocks will be run.

To fix these conflicts, you have to remove the common overlap between rules. For example, the correct way to do such a list is the following:

```
optional_list:
  %empty
  | optional_list item
  ;
```

Bison's default resolution to reduce/reduce conflicts is to choose the rule that appears first, which is obviously dangerous when anyone shuffles code around.

3.1.5 Reading conflict messages

Even if you have a good grasp on shift/reduce and reduce/reduce conflicts, you have one more hurdle: understanding how to read Bison's conflict messages.

Here is a minimal example of a shift/reduce conflict for a non-ambiguous language:

```
%token A B C
%%
top:
  %empty
  | top A
  | top A B
  | top B C
```

The core conflict comes from having read A and seeing that B is next; Bison could either reduce the single A in the hope that B is part of "B C", or it could shift the B and reduce "A B". Let's see how the .output file reports this to us.

The first line helpfully tells us which state has the problem:

```
State 3 conflicts: 1 shift/reduce
```

The next section is a Grammar summary listing rules and their numbers, followed by list of Terminal symbols, followed by a list of Nonterminal symbols. Then we get to the important part - the list of States. The first state is always looking for the top rule; here is what it is for this example:

```
State 0
    0 $accept:  . top $end
    $default    reduce using rule 1 (top)
    top   go to state 1
```

Each line that starts with a number is a grammar
rule that this state applies to. Here we have only one ("0"),
and since this is the top-rule it has two special elements in
it: $accept is a special symbol that is reached when the
input matches the grammar, and $end represents the end
of input. Between those, we see "." and "top". "." is a
marker to say where this state is in the input stream. In
this case, there is nothing to the left (which means we have
not seen anything yet) and "top" on the right (which
means it is the next thing this rule expects to see).

The remaining lines indicate what will happen
when various possible things are seen next. $default
means this rule could be empty and none of the others
match, so in that case it will reduce. "top" is the name of
our top-level rule, and if that is seen next, then Bison will
go to state 1.

Let's jump to State 3, where the reported conflict
was:

```
State 3
    2 top: top A .
    3    | top A . B
    B   shift, and go to state 5
    B             [reduce using rule 2
(top)]
    $default    reduce using rule 2 (top)
```

Here there are two rules mentioned (2 and 3),
which means with the current input we have not yet
figured out which applies. The left side of the marker (".")

will always be the same in any one State, and here we see that we have seen an input of just A[37].

The next line indicates that if it sees an input of B that it should shift (keep looking) and go to state 5. We can read ahead to see that State 5 simply reduces "top A B" down to "top", so it matches our "top ::= top A B" rule.

The very next line in State 3, however, also looks for an input of B, and this is the basis of our problem. This rule wants to reduce instead of shift (hence a "shift/reduce" conflict). It reduces using rule 2, which is our "top ::= top A" rule.

To finish diagnosing the conflict, we would like to know what Bison might do after the reduction, so that we can figure out the ambiguous situation. However, you will notice that reductions do not indicate which state it goes to next, but rather the nonterminal symbol they reduce. For this example, it is top. So now we look for where in our grammar we have a top followed by a B. This is trivial here because we have a literal rule (top ::= top B C), but in general top could have been followed by a nonterminal that starts with a B, and there is no indication in .output of where to start looking. Debugging shift/reduce conflicts can occasionally be painful.

Reduce/reduce conflicts are usually easier to diagnose. Let's consider this even smaller minimal example:

---

[37] Well, top A, but top is a recursive rule that could be empty, so it does not help us find problematic input sequences.

```
%token A
%%
top:
  A
  | A
  ;
```

stdout tells us there is a reduce/reduce conflict, as does the header of the .output report:

```
State 1 conflicts: 1 reduce/reduce
```

Looking at State 1, we see:

```
State 1
     1 top: A .
     2    | A .
     $end       reduce using rule 1 (top)
     $end       [reduce using rule 2
(top)]
     $default  reduce using rule 1 (top)
```

Here we see the two rules involved (1 and 2), and that alone is usually enough to help you locate the source of your problem.

Again we see that Bison put the unused action's text in brackets to indicate that it chose a different action in this ambiguous situation. The brackets are a good visual marker to look for when perusing .output for issues.

If none of the above made sense, review chapter 7 of *Flex & Bison* for a second opinion on reading .output files.[38]

---

[38] I guess technically it is the first opinion.

3.1.6 Overcoming the one-symbol lookahead limit

Bison's lookahead limit of only one symbol will cause the occasional headache. Though you cannot always get around it, there are some tricks to try before you resort to turning on GLR mode.[39]

We can use precedence to resolve shift/reduce conflicts, and precedence works by comparing the precedence of the rule to the precedence of the next token, but what if the next token is unhelpful and the actual precedence comes from the token after it? A contrived example might be an expression grammar that encodes comments:

```
%token COMMENT
%token NUM
%left COMMENT
%left '+'
%left '*'
%%
expr:
  NUM
  | expr opt_comment '+' expr
  | expr opt_comment '*' expr
  ;
opt_comment:
  %empty
  | COMMENT
  ;
```

Even with %left set up correctly, the existence of opt_comment here generates 4 reduce/reduce conflicts, and destroys mathematical precedence. (And note that we had to set the associativity and precedence for COMMENT, to avoid its shift/reduce conflicts.)

---

[39] See §3.5.1 for additional notes on GLR.

A solution here is to change the grammar so that next tokens always have a precedence. Specifically, we could factor out expr COMMENT to turn it into a single nonterminal in the other rules:

```
%token COMMENT
%token NUM
%left COMMENT
%left '+'
%left '*'
%%
expr:
  NUM
  | expr COMMENT
  | expr '+' expr
  | expr '*' expr
  ;
```

A related idea for reducing the symbol count is to combine multiple symbols in Flex instead of Bison. To reuse an example from the previous section:

```
%token A B C

%%

top:
  %empty
  | top A
  | top B
  | top A B C
  ;
```

This presents one shift/reduce conflict, but we could resolve that if we change Flex to return "A B C" as a single token instead of as three tokens:

```
    // Flex patterns:
[ \t]  ;
A { return A; }
B { return B; }
A[ \t]+B[ \t]+C { return ABC; }

    // Bison rules:
%token A B ABC
%%
top:
  %empty
  | top A
  | top B
  | top ABC
  ;
```

Of course, this assumes that the token/nonterminal values can be combined (and possibly recovered!), which is application dependent. It also assumes the only things between A, B, and C will be spaces and tabs (copy-pasted from the whitespace pattern!), which leaves newlines and inlined comments unsupported.

Flex & Bison mentions another Flex-based solution to this situation, and it avoids copy-pasting the whitespace pattern. Assuming your grammar never needs any of the initial tokens in a given sequence, you could refrain from returning them, and use Flex to keep track of what has been seen. You could keep track with either global variables or with start states. The global variable approach might look like this:

```
// Flex patterns:
C {
   last_was_c = 1;
   // no return
}
D {
   if (last_was_c) {
      last_was_c = 0;
      return C_and_D;
   }
    else { … }
}
E {
   if (last_was_c) {
      last_was_c = 0;
      return C_and_E;
   }
   else { … }
}

// Bison rules:
top: A B {…} C_and_D
  | A B {…} C_and_E
  ;
```

An alternative that does not rely on globals uses start-states instead, for a more elegant solution:

```
// Flex patterns:
C  {
   yy_push_state(EXPECTING_D_OR_E);
}
<EXPECTING_D_OR_E>D   {
   yy_pop_state();
   return C_and_D;
}
<EXPECTING_D_OR_E>E   {
   yy_pop_state();
   return C_and_E;
}
```

A final obscure cause of one-symbol-lookahead conflicts is the location of code blocks within the grammar. Bison must have code blocks at the end of rules, and as a convenience it will automatically break apart any rules with code blocks. Thus the following:

```
top: A B {…} C ;
```

is internally broken up into:

```
top: r142 C ;
r142: A B {…} ;
```

This can create a reduce/reduce conflict where there would not normally be one:

```
top: A B {…} C D
   | A B {…} C E
   ;
```

To resolve this, try to keep your code blocks as far to the end as possible. Even shifting over by one is enough to resolve this example, since D and E are unique:

```
top: A B C {…} D
   | A B C {…} E
   ;
```

If the code itself happens to be the exact same in all the rules, then an even better solution is to reduce code duplication by factoring out the common part:

```
top: A B C {…} ending ;
ending: D | E ;
```

3.2 Functionality and correctness

3.2.1 Beware of lookahead when controlling the lexer

The ability for Bison to control Flex is occasionally useful, as it lets the parser provide some context to the lexer. But as we noticed in §3.1.6, code blocks may be stepped over to resolve a reduce/reduce conflict, so the lexer might not have been controlled after all.

Consider a possible variable declaration statement that creates a variable of a given type and initial value, except that this language puts the initial value before the type:

```
declare myvar1 5 int
declare myvar2 42 float
```

The straightforward definition of the tokens and grammar will not work:

```
    // Flex patterns:
declare             { return DECLARE; }
float               { return FLOAT; }
int                 { return INT; }
[0-9]+              { return INTNUM; }
[0-9]+\.?[0-9]+     { return FLOATNUM; }
[a-zA-Z_][a-zA-Z0-9_]*  {
                    return IDENT; }

    // Bison rules:
declare:
        DECLARE ident INTNUM INT
      | DECLARE ident FLOATNUM FLOAT
    ;
```

Since 42 happens to match the patterns for both INTNUM and FLOATNUM, the tie is broken in favor of

123

INTNUM (listed first), which makes Bison think we are building the declare: DECLARE ident INTNUM INT rule, and then the subsequent float generates a parse error.

To resolve this, we might try to have Bison tell Flex that the next number it sees is a FLOATNUM even if it looks like an INTNUM:

```
declare:
      DECLARE ident INTNUM INT
    | DECLARE ident
      { force_float(); }
      FLOATNUM FLOAT
    ;
```

force_float is a function we will write that tells Flex that the next thing it sees is a FLOATNUM. If we were to implement it using start-states, our Flex file might look like this:

```
// Make an exclusive state in order
// to avoid the INTNUM pattern:
%x FORCEFLOAT
...
%%
...
<FORCEFLOAT>[0-9]+\.?[0-9]*   {
    yy_pop_state();
    return FLOATNUM;
  }
%%
void force_float() {
  yy_push_state(FORCEFLOAT);
}
```

Unfortunately this does not actually solve the problem. The fact that Bison has to decide whether to run the { force_float(); } code block requires it to fetch the next lookahead token, which is going to be parsed normally. Thus, 42 still shows up as an INTNUM, and the code block is not run, even *after* we wanted it to be run.

In the general case, there is no silver-bullet solution to this problem. However, there are still a few tricks to try.

First, the most obvious solution for this example is to tell the grammar that an INTNUM is also acceptable in a FLOAT definition:

```
declare:
      DECLARE ident INTNUM INT
    | DECLARE ident FLOATNUM FLOAT
    | DECLARE ident INTNUM FLOAT
    ;
```

This may or may not be feasible depending on your grammar - it implies that every use of FLOATNUM in your language requires a copy-pasted rule to also accept INTNUM instead.

Second, you might try to eliminate the need for a lookahead. Here, we could replace both FLOATNUM and INTNUM with a generic NUM that we resolve later:

```
// Only one Flex pattern for both now:
[0-9]+\.?[0-9]*   { return NUM; }

// Bison changes:
%token NUM
...
%%
declare:
    DECLARE IDENT NUM INT
  | DECLARE IDENT NUM FLOAT
  ;
```

Note, however, that this change flipped the grammar from failing on a false negative (an error using an INTNUM to declare a float) to allowing a false positive (using a FLOATNUM to declare an int). The user code for the int rule would need to check for that and decide if that is an error.

However, the final refinement of this idea is to add a rule matching either INTNUM or FLOATNUM:

```
// Flex patterns:
declare           { return DECLARE; }
float             { return FLOAT; }
int               { return INT; }
[0-9]+            { return INTNUM; }
[0-9]+\.?[0-9]+   { return FLOATNUM; }
[a-zA-Z_][a-zA-Z0-9_]*  {
                    return IDENT; }

// Bison rules:
int_or_float: INTNUM | FLOATNUM ;

declare:
      DECLARE ident INTNUM INT
    | DECLARE ident int_or_float FLOAT
    ;
```

This avoids having to deal with either start-states or user code blocks, and also does not let a FLOATNUM be used in an INT declaration.

3.2.2 Check to make sure all your tokens are generated by Flex

There should be a one-to-one correlation between the set of tokens returned by Flex patterns and the set of tokens declared in the Bison grammar[40]. Happily, if a Flex pattern returns a token type that is not defined by Bison, it will generate a compilation error in the Flex unit, because the identifier is unknown.

However, the inverse is not true. If Bison defines a token that is never returned by Flex, there is no compile-time indication at all. There is at least a run-time indication — since the token will never be returned by Flex, any rule that needs it will throw a parse error on whatever token it did see. But this can still be rather annoying to debug, since your grammar and input could otherwise align perfectly.

Regrettably, I know of no automated way to ensure that all tokens are returned by at least one Flex pattern.

---

[40] Remember that Bison declares tokens with %token, %precedence, %left, %right, and %nonassoc.

3.2.3 Enable mid-rule action warnings

Mid-rule actions have values just like tokens, and there are two helpful warnings Bison can issue about potential problems with them. First, it can detect that you tried to use a value without defining it. For example:

```
myrule: A {} B {
    printf("%d\n", $2);
  } ;
```

Here, $2 refers to the value of the code block between A and B, but the code block does not set $$.

Second, you could do the exact opposite — define the value for a code block but never use it:

```
myrule: A { $$ = 1; } B ;
```

Both of those situations can be detected by enabling warnings on the Bison command line:

```
-Wmidrule-value
--warnings=midrule-value
```

These generate non-fatal warnings:

```
warning: unset value: $$ [-Wmidrule-
values]
  myrule: A {} B {
             ^^

...
warning: unused value: $2 [-Wmidrule-
values]
  myrule: A { $$ = 1; } B ;
            ^^^^^^^^^^^
```

3.2.4 Handling contextual precedence

Precedence is an elegant mechanism for resolving shift/reduce conflicts, but one important wrinkle is that an operator's precedence can occasionally depend on context. The example from section 5.4 of the Bison manual is the hyphen, which has high precedence when used for unary negation and lower precedence when used in subtraction.

To illustrate the core problem, consider the following simple expression:

```
2^-2*3
```

(Where ^ is exponentiation and has higher precedence than both addition and multiplication.) This could be grouped in two ways:

- (2 ^ (-2)) * 3, yielding 3/4.
- (2 ^ (-2 * 3)), yielding 1/64.

While there is some debate about the correct interpretation[41], the consensus seems to be tilting towards the first. In order for that to work, the precedence of - has to be higher than * so that Bison will reduce the -2 instead of shifting the 2*3.

The implementation is to override the rule's precedence using %prec. The Bison manual's example illustrates how to handle this with an artificial high-precedence UMINUS symbol:

---

[41] Math itself is not ambiguous; what is ambiguous is the serialization of math operations in text format in programming languages.

```
%left '-' '+'
%left '*' '/'
%right '^'
%left UMINUS
...
exp:
    ...
  | exp '-' exp
  | '-' exp %prec UMINUS
  | exp '^' exp
```

UMINUS is declared last (giving it the highest precedence), and the rule using "-" for negation overrides -'s default low precedence.

3.2.5 Dealing with %locations

Technically, there is no requirement that a single token be restricted to a single line. A quoted string, for example, could include embedded carriage returns, and thus the beginning and end of the string have different line numbers. Relying on just yylineno for error reporting then does not give us the complete picture. Instead, each token has a starting line number and ending line number.

Taking this idea one step farther, each token also has a starting column and an ending column, so to fully capture the location of a token we have four data fields. For most applications, deriving and storing this information is overkill, but sometimes it is helpful, such as for error messages that want to indicate more than just a line number for parse errors — for example, you could print a row of carets underneath the original source line to indicate exactly where in the line a problem is.

The first step to enabling locations is the Bison directive %locations. This creates the YYLTYPE struct like so:

```
typedef struct YYLTYPE {
  int first_line;
  int first_column;
  int last_line;
  int last_column;
} YYLTYPE;
```

It also creates a global variable of this type named yylloc. As covered in §2.5.6, Flex does not always automatically track line numbers for you very well, and it turns out it does not track column numbers at all. You will need to have your Flex code update yylloc for each token. There are a few different approaches, but most straightforward is to leverage `YY_USER_ACTION` to update it. Our approach will update the fields so that `first_line` and `first_column` are the location of the first character of the token, and `last_line` and `last_column` are the first character *after* the token. Note that we will make all numbers 1-based instead of 0-based, so the first row and first column are both number 1.

```
%{
#include "template.tab.h"

void update_yylloc() {
  // This token's start is where the
  // last one ended:
  yylloc.first_line = yylloc.last_line;
  yylloc.first_column =
yylloc.last_column;
  // To find this token's end we have to
  // account for carriage returns in
  // yytext:
  for(int i = 0;
      yytext[i] != '\0';
      ++i) {
    if(yytext[i] == '\n') {
      yylloc.last_line++;
      yylloc.last_column = 1;
    }
    else {
      yylloc.last_column++;
    }
  }
}

#define YY_USER_ACTION update_yylloc();

%}
%%
...
```

This works fine for basic lexers, but there are some

caveats to be aware of as you become more sophisticated.

First, if your lexer must also support a `#include`-like mechanism, you will need to update the code from §2.4.7 to save and restore `yylloc` instead of just `yylineno`.

Second, if you have enabled reentrancy with `%define api.pure full`, then you have a few changes to deal with:

- Flex's `%option bison-bridge` is changed to `%option bison-locations` (which implies `%option bison-bridge` and adds a `yylex` argument for location information).
- Our `update_yylloc` function cannot access `yytext` anymore. Ostensibly that should be because `yytext` is a global variable that gets encapsulated by turning on pure parsing, but the real reason is that Flex's convenient `#define` of `yytext` that would allow continued use is inconveniently placed after the user code. Thus, we have to declare and call the `yyget_text` function.
- Our call to `update_yyloc` needs a `yyscan_t` argument.
- The Flex functions we declare from Bison now also have `yyscan_t` arguments.

Here is a minimal example I got working with both reentrancy and locations:

```
  // Flex:
%option reentrant
%option bison-locations

%{
#include "template.tab.h"
char *yyget_text(yyscan_t);

void update_yylloc(YYLTYPE *yylloc,
    yyscan_t yyscanner) {
  // This token's start is where the
  // last one ended:
  yylloc->first_line =
      yylloc->last_line;
  yylloc->first_column =
      yylloc->last_column;

  // To find this token's end we have to
  // account for carriage returns in
  // yytext.  To get to yytext when
  // we've enabled a pure parser, we
  // have to use a function:
  char *yyt = yyget_text(yyscanner);

  for(int i = 0;
      yyt[i] != '\0';
      ++i) {
    if(yyt[i] == '\n') {
      yylloc->last_line++;
      yylloc->last_column = 1;
    }
    else {
      yylloc->last_column++;
    }
  }
}

#define YY_USER_ACTION \
    update_yylloc(yylloc, yyscanner);

%}
%%
```

```
// Bison:
%code top {
typedef void *yyscan_t;
}


%code provides {
#include <stdio.h>
#include <stdlib.h>

extern void yyset_in(FILE*, yyscan_t);
extern int yylex(YYSTYPE*, YYLTYPE*,
    yyscan_t);
extern int yylex_init(yyscan_t*);
extern int yylex_destroy(yyscan_t);
extern int yyparse(yyscan_t);

void yyerror(yyscan_t, YYLTYPE*,
    const char *);
}

%locations
%define api.pure full
%lex-param {yyscan_t this_scanner}
%parse-param {yyscan_t this_scanner}

%%
```

A note on performance: much as we have to compute terminal symbol locations with our update_yylloc function, Bison has to compute *non*terminal symbol locations, which it does on every reduction. Though it is a simple operation, the Bison documentation notes that this extra processing can make the parser noticeably slower.

3.2.6 Avoid YYBACKUP

YYBACKUP is Bison's equivalent to Flex's yyless — it allows you to inject an arbitrary token into the input stream, to control what the tool sees next. There are substantial limitations when it can be used:

- it can only be used in rules that reduce one single token,
- it cannot be used if Bison happened to need a lookahead token to find the rule,
- it cannot be used in GLR parsers at all.

Given how difficult it is to assure all of the above (especially controlling when a lookahead is needed), it is best to try to avoid YYBACKUP completely.

3.2.7 Using Flex/Bison with readline

readline is a nifty library that provides line editing, command completion, and history for interactive terminal programs. Using it with Flex and Bison obviously means we will use string input instead of file input, but that is not quite enough. The trick for getting it to work is to swap buffers so that each line is treated as complete input.

The changes to the yyparse invocation are straightforward:

```
char *line;
while ((line = readline("% "))) {
  YY_BUFFER_STATE buff
    = yy_scan_string(line);
  yy_switch_to_buffer(buff);
  yyparse();
  yy_delete_buffer(buff);
}
```

Slightly less straightforward is dealing with the fact that these are all Flex functions. In order to avoid having to #include Flex's generated header file, I added the following declarations:

```
#include "readline/readline.h"
typedef struct yy_buffer_state
  *YY_BUFFER_STATE;

void
yy_switch_to_buffer(YY_BUFFER_STATE);

void
yy_delete_buffer(YY_BUFFER_STATE);

YY_BUFFER_STATE
yy_scan_string(const char *);
```

The final binary will need to be linked with the
`readline` library as well, though your specific `#include`
and linking will depend on your platform and project.

3.3 Efficiency

3.3.1 Use left recursion (instead of right recursion)

To support arbitrary pattern repetition, Bison allows you to specify rules recursively. The following rule matches 0 or more FOO elements:

```
foos:
  %empty
  | FOO foos ;
```

It reads easily to humans: "the rule foos could be either nothing, or it could be a FOO followed by more foos." However, this rule is terrible for Bison, because it cannot start reducing the second rule until it sees the *entire* list. Consequently, all of the FOOs in an arbitrarily long sequence pile up on Bison's internal stack. This is *right recursion*, so-called because the recursive element (foos) is on the right end of the recursive rule (foos: FOO foos).

In *left recursion*, the order is reversed:

```
foos:
  %empty
  | foos FOO ;
```

This is a little harder for humans, but substantially easier for Bison. The stack of FOOs only grows to one before Bison can reduce the second rule, so this will not blow up Bison's stack.

Another benefit to left recursion is that it preserves the order of the input, whereas right recursion reverses it. In a real application, you may be adding FOOs to a list in a parse tree, but suppose we merely print them:

```
// With right-recursion:
foos:
  %empty
  | FOO foos { printf("%s\n", $1); } ;

// With left-recursion:
foos:
  %empty
  | foos FOO { printf("%s\n", $2); } ;
```

With left recursion, the rule is reduced after each FOO is seen, and so each printf happens in order.

With right recursion, the rule is reduced only when all of the FOOs have been seen, which means the one being reduced is actually the *last* one in the series. Thus the last one is printed first, and so on.

3.4 Maintenance

3.4.1 Upgrade `yyerror`

For error reporting, the lowest-hanging fruit is to redefine the default `yyerror` function, which (as *Flex & Bison* points out) is so trivial that we can print it in its entirety here to show you how little information it conveys:

```
void yyerror(char *errmsg) {
  fprintf(stderr, "%s\n", errmsg);
}
```

`errmsg` is usually set to simply "`syntax error`", so you can see its usefulness is limited.

The most basic helpful additions to this message are:

- the current file name. Unfortunately Bison does not have the slightest idea what file is being read, so you have to handle this yourself.
- the current line number. This may be in `yylineno`, assuming you have enabled it and your Flex rules have been updating it.
- the current token (in `yytext`).

(You may decide you also want to include the lookahead token. It is available in `yyname[yychar]`, but only if you enable `%token-table`. Additionally, `yychar` contains a Bison token number, but that could be either `YYEOF` (if you are at the end of the input) or `YYEMPTY` (if a lookahead did not happen to be needed). You should check those conditions before using it in `yyname`.)

Of the elements we would like to include in error messages, only `yytext` is consistently available in `yyerror`. Both file name and line number are application specific - you may have global variables for them, or you may have a stack of them for supporting `#includes`.

Without stacks, adding a global variable for the file name is easy:

```
%{
#include <string.h>
...
// Defined by Flex:
extern int yylineno;
extern char *yytext;
// Locally defined:
char *mysrcfile=0;
void yyerror(const char *);
%}
%%
...
%%
int main(int argc, char **argc) {
  ...
  yyin = fopen(argv[1], "r");
  ...
  mysrcfile = strdup(argv[1]);
  ...
  yyparse();
  ...
}

void yyerror(const char *msg) {
  printf("%s on '%s': line %d of %s\n",
      msg, yytext, yylineno,
      mysrcfile);
}
```

The stack case was touched on in §2.4.7, but

assuming you have a similar configuration, then your version of yyerror would get the file name from the stack instead:

```
void yyerror(const char *msg) {
  printf("%s on '%s': line %d of %s\n",
    msg, yytext, yylineno,
    bufstack->filename);
}
```

Another possible upgrade is to report the entire line that contains the error. *Flex & Bison* explores this on page 199 - it has Flex store each line by capturing the carriage return first and calling yyless(1) to resume normal lexing. Then, yyerror can print the last captured line to provide the user with context.

A final update is to report a fixed number of errors before halting. Bison keeps track of the number of times it has called yyerror in the global variable yynerrs, so all you need to do is compare it to your limit before halting for real. Note that you cannot use YYABORT inside yyerror, so you have to issue a hard stop with exit (or abort).

```
void yyerror(const char *msg) {
  printf("Error number %d:\n", yynerrs);
  ...
  if (yynerrs == 10) {
    exit(-1);
  }
}
```

Remember to check yynerrs right after calling yyparse, in case the number of errors was less than your limit. Also, if you call yyerror yourself directly, you will need to increment yynerrs yourself as well.

Lastly, note that the signature of `yyerror` changes if you enabled both locations (`%locations`) and reentrancy (`%define api.pure full`) to include a pointer to a `YYLTYPE` object:

```
void yyerror(YYLTYPE *, char const *);
```

3.4.2 Implement error checking

The single best return on investment for reducing maintenance is to implement good error checking and reporting. For your users, a clear, accurate message tells them what the immediate problem is and how to fix it — which prevents them from having to ask you. For you, a clear, accurate message about an internal error describes the disconnect — which does a lot of diagnosis you would have had to perform.

One way to handle syntax errors is through "error productions", where you explicitly match bad input. Consider the following rules to catch when users forget a semicolon at the end of an assignment statement:

```
assign:
   identifier '=' expression ';' {
      ...
   }
 | identifier '=' expression {
      yyerror("missing ':'");
      ...
   }
 ;
```

This has several advantages:
• the error message tells the user specifically what the problem is.
• Bison can continue on without cascaded errors, allowing you to list multiple problems in a single pass.

There is the disadvantage that all those extra rules grow the size of the parsing tables; your project's constraints will determine how acceptable the empirical impact is. Another disadvantage is that this introduces a possibly significant amount of copy-pasted rules.

Another way to handle syntax errors is the special error keyword in Bison, which is matched when nothing else is. The specific point of the error keyword is to try to get Bison back on track so that it can find the next real problem (as opposed to a cascaded problem). Consider again the assignment statement example, except now maybe it is the expression part that is syntactically incorrect. In this scenario, we use error to ignore everything until the next semicolon, and then resume parsing as if everything were okay:

```
assign:
  identifier '=' expression ';'
  | identifier '=' error ';'
  ;
```

Note that this does not *waive* errors — Bison still calls yyerror, and yynerrs is still incremented.

Now that we have one solution for input missing a semicolon and one solution for input mangling the syntax of an expression, an obvious followup question is, what if the input did both? Unfortunately, we have pretty much reached the limit for meeting the user halfway with syntax errors. There is a practical limit to how far to take error recovery before encountering diminishing returns.

A further consideration using error is freeing memory in discarded tokens. error works by discarding input tokens until it finds something it recognizes (in the above example, that is the ';' we put after error). But since the tokens are discarded, no grammar rules will have the ability to free any memory allocated for them. This concern is particularly relevant if your application is an interactive command line, which can continue running for an arbitrary amount of time with an arbitrary number of

146

user-generated errors. Thus, we have Bison's
%destructor declaration, which lets you define a block
of code for each token type to free its resources:

```
    // Flex:
%%
[a-zA-Z]+   {
    yylval.sval = strdup(yytext);
    return STR;
}
%%

    // Bison:
%union {
    char *sval;
}

%token <sval> STR
%destructor { free($$); } STR
%%
%%
```

Note that Bison supports %destructor for tokens
and nonterminals, but not for arbitrary mid-rule actions. If
you need to ensure that you free that memory as well, try
splitting the rule so that the mid-rule action becomes an
end-rule action; at that point the rule is now a new
nonterminal, and you can define its %destructor as
usual.

If your program is going to try to reparse instead of
completely exiting, a final consideration is cleaning up
Bison's state after fatal errors. Use yyclearin to flush the
inputs, and remember to reset Flex's state as well with
yy_flush_buffer and START(INITIAL).

A final endorsement: error only incurs a runtime
penalty if it is actually used; in correct input, it adds no

147

overhead.

For more information, *Flex & Bison* covers error recovery extensively in chapter 8.

3.4.3 Use precedence to resolve dangling else

The "dangling else" problem can be resolved in a few ways, but the best choice (when possible) is explicitly raising the precedence of the rule that has the else. That resolves the inherent shift/reduce conflict in favor of the shift (which is Bison's default, but it is good to remove the warning).

```
%left IF
%left ELSE
%%

stmt:
  if_stmt
  | ...
  ;

if_stmt:
  IF expr stmt     %prec IF
  | IF expr stmt ELSE stmt
  ;
```

Another way (discussed on page 188 of *Flex & Bison*) is to rewrite the grammar so that it is forced to shift. This idea is to not have the same stmt nonterminal in both cases, and to ensure that the nonterminal before ELSE cannot be produced by an IF without an ELSE. Easier said than done - it is quite a brain teaser to work through this solution. If-without-else is still a statement, but now it is one that can no longer be matched everywhere that our grammar currently allows stmt. Thus we end up dividing our statement rules between one statement nonterminal that can be used in one context and a different statement nonterminal that can be used in other contexts. *Flex & Bison* calls them matched (for if-with-else, and all other usual statements we had in stmt such as assignment) and unmatched (for if-without-else). In our if-with-else rule, the nonterminal before `ELSE` is changed to `matched` so that it can no longer match if-without-else. Our progress so far:

```
stmt:
  matched
  | unmatched
  ;

matched:
  ...usual statement rules...
  | IF expr matched ELSE matched
  ;

unmatched:
  IF expr stmt
  ;
```

Notice that we did not replace `stmt` with `matched` and `unmatched` but rather added them as rules that reduce to `stmt`. This allows our if-without-else rule to continue using `stmt` instead of needing two rules (one to match `IF expr matched` and one for `IF expr unmatched`.)

Also notice that we changed the `stmt` *after* `ELSE` to `matched`; without that, we end up with the exact same shift/reduce conflict we started out trying to avoid. However, that means this grammar now cannot match an if-with-else whose `ELSE` statement is an if-without-else.

We need a corresponding `IF expr matched ELSE unmatched` rule. Since such a rule absolutely cannot be followed by an `ELSE`, we cannot have it reduce to `matched`, or else it creates the shift/reduce conflict again with our other if-with-else statement. Instead, we reduce it to `unmatched`[42], giving us the final grammar-massaging solution to the dangling-else problem:

```
stmt:
  matched
  | unmatched
  ;

matched:
  ...usual statement rules...
  | IF expr matched ELSE matched
  ;

unmatched:
  IF expr stmt
  | IF expr matched ELSE unmatched
  ;
```

Of these two solutions, *Flex & Bison* suggests the latter, but I stick with the former. The rearrangement of the rules makes them unintuitive to read — you saw how much text I used just to try to explain how it works. But it is also fairly fragile, so the first strategy has better maintainability.

---

[42] Which makes sense; `unmatched` was created specifically for an `IF` that cannot be followed by an `ELSE`, and that is also true for this rule.

3.4.4 Do not put more than you can into the grammar

It is a good idea to push as much functionality as you can into the grammar (as opposed to doing it yourself in code blocks). Bison is brilliant at tasks like matching parentheses and building a hierarchical parse tree. However, there is a limit, and some situations are best *not* handled by Bison. For example, checking identifiers to ensure type consistency is best done as a post-processing step on your final syntax tree. Consider an attempt to type-check integer declarations by allowing it to match only integer-yielding expressions:

```
INT ident '=' int_expr ';'
```

We can match `int_expr` to integer constants easily, but as we handle other types of expressions this becomes unwieldy. Variables require that we look them up in a symbol table to assert that they are also `INT`s; or if the other variable's type is not primitive, we may require a class hierarchy so that we can assert that it inherits from `INT`. Or more painfully, maybe the language allows typecasting, and then we have to see if there is a usable typecast operator to `INT`.[43] Moving beyond assignments variables, assignments to the output of a function implies that Bison would have to support different nonterminals for functions depending on their return type (say, `int_function_call`). And that runs into similar problems — if a function returns a class that inherits from `INT`, how would Bison know whether to consider it an `int_function_call` so that it could be used in integer assignments? Finally, consider how you would enforce

---

[43] Worse, not all languages require declaration before use, so we might not yet have either a complete symbol table or a class hierarchy.

type checking with user-defined types, for which you cannot write Bison rules ahead of time. You would be forced to generalize them all (e.g. `generic_function_call`) and sort it out procedurally (e.g. this context expects type A and this token is type B; figure out if they are somehow compatible). Hopefully this rambling (and decisively incomplete) discussion illustrates how much type checking is better handled as a post-processing step than directly baked in a parser.

Another problem best not solved in a Bison grammar is ensuring that the number of arguments passed to a function is correct[44]. You may be tempted, for example, to specify that your built-in square-root function takes exactly one argument:

```
sqrt_function: SQRT '(' argument ')' ';'
```

This would indeed generate parser-level errors if anyone attempts to call it with two arguments, but consider the message generated — it would complain about a syntax error with ')'. A generalized validator might complain about having too many arguments in the function call, which is much more helpful to the user. Also, consider that enforcing an argument count in your grammar means you would have to define every one of your primitives in the grammar. This is another case where it is more effective to *not* implement something in a Bison grammar.

A final example is array index checking. Unlike the previous examples, the essence of this problem is that it

----

[44] I specifically mean built-in functions. User-defined functions have an arbitrary number of arguments, and anything user-defined cannot be codified in the language grammar anyway.

can only be solved at run-time. That is, while the index could be a literal integer, it could also be the value of a variable or the return value from a function. The specific value cannot be determined until the program is run, which is long after the grammar is compiled.

In general, any situation that requires runtime data cannot be solved in a Bison grammar.

See also §3.6.2 ("Avoid trying to perfectly handle unordered lists").

3.4.5 Do not create your own numeric code for tokens

By default, Bison autogenerates numeric codes for tokens, which guarantees that they will never conflict. The only good reason for specifying your own numeric token code is to be compatible with an existing lexer you cannot change.

You can see the numeric codes generated for the tokens in the `tab.h` file generated by Bison's `-d` switch; look for the `yytokentype` enum. You will notice they start on a high number (258, currently) — this is so that individual characters can use their ASCII number as their token value without requiring declaration in Bison. That is, you do not need "`%token =`" or "`%token ;`" to be able to use them in rules:

```
assign: lvalue '=' expr ';'
```

You would have to go to extra effort to define your own numeric values for tokens; I mention this only in preparation for the next tip.

3.4.6 Define text for literal strings tokens

Single-character constant tokens (for example, most punctuation characters) are commonly used in Bison grammars literally. Bison uses their ASCII value as the token number, and since Flex returns them directly, there is a clean handoff between them.

Less common is multi-character constant tokens, such as == or . *. Flex cannot return these directly (they are strings instead of characters), so it takes a little effort to enable this mechanism. First, Bison has to declare them as a proper token, though it also specifies the string value:

```
%token EQ "=="
```

The Flex pattern looks the same as usual - it matches == and return EQ as the token type:

```
==   { return EQ; }
```

But now your grammar may use "==" as a token, similar to how it may use '=' or '+':

```
eq_check: expr "==" expr ;
```

One additional benefit of doing this is that Bison's debug messages print the string value instead of the token name, which makes the output a little more intuitive to read. After enabling debugging with both %define parse.trace and yydebug=1, the debugging output changes from this:

```
Reading a token: Next token is token EQ
()
```

To this:

```
Reading a token: Next token is token
"==" ()
```

Be careful to not redefine the token's numeric value at the same time (see previous tip), which is also done with extra arguments to %token. However, one exception is that you may want to give a value for the END token so that debugging messages say something other than $end to mean end-of-file. Since this redefines a built-in token, in this case you do need to specify its value, which is zero:

```
%token END 0 "end of file"
```

It remains to be seen if changing this output:

```
Shifting token $end ()
```

To this:

```
Shifting token "end of file" ()
```

Justifies the extra effort.

A final note if the token needs a declared associativity or precedence. The syntax for %left/ %right/%precedence is not the same as %token's, and does not let you specify a token name at all:

```
%left "=="
```

By itself, that is not enough, because Flex has to return EQ. The solution is to have both %token and %left declarations:

```
%token EQ "=="
%left "=="
```

3.4.7 Avoid `%expect` and `%expect-rr`

`%expect` and `%expect-rr` let you declare how many shift-reduce and reduce-reduce conflicts you expect in the grammar. This is essentially a waiver mechanism for Bison's warnings, but it is dangerous — since it uses only the count of the warnings and not the actual warnings themselves, it is entirely possible that an errant change could "resolve" one conflict but create another, effectively waiving a new problem.

The best practice is to resolve all the conflict warnings, of course. See §3.1.3 ("Understanding shift/reduce conflicts"), §3.1.4 ("Understanding reduce/reduce conflicts"), and §3.4.3 ("Use precedence to resolve dangling else") for a few tips on eliminating them. The easiest path for fixing these is when you happen to have control over the language, though typically you do not. Still, there are still some surprising tricks grammars can employ.

3.4.8 Consider using named references

Bison allows you to associate names with rule elements, so that instead of using $N you can use more meaningful names that are easier to understand later. For example, consider a possible definition of a function call statement:

```
stmt:
   ident '(' expr ')' {
     $$ = call_func($1, $3);
   }
```

You could specify meaningful names:

```
stmt[func]:
   ident[name] '(' expr[arg] ')' {
     $[func] = call_func($[name], $
[arg]);
   }
```

In addition to being (mostly) clearer to read, this comes with the much more substantial benefit of being more resilient to updates. That is, if someday this rule was updated to require an explicit call keyword:

```
stmt[func]:
   CALL ident[name] '(' expr[arg] ')' {
     $[func] = call_func($[name],
        $[arg]);
   }
```

This rule would continue to work, whereas the implementation using $1 and $3 would now be trying to use the values of the CALL token and an open parenthesis.

This syntax lets you define any names you want for nonterminals in the rule, and this gives you support for having more than one of the same type:

```
stmt[func]:
    CALL ident[name] '(' expr[arg1] ','
expr[arg2] ')' {
        $[func] = call_func($[name],
            $[arg1], $[arg2]);
    }
```

Even better, there are some syntactic shortcuts you may take with these named references. First is that the brackets in the code block are only required if the name has periods, hyphens, or other characters which may cause Bison some parsing confusion. Thus, our one-argument function call example could also be written like this:

```
stmt[func]:
    CALL ident[name] '(' expr[arg] ')' {
        $func = call_func($name, $arg);
    }
```

The second shortcut is that if a nonterminal in your rule has unique name within that rule, you could use that name instead of giving it a new name string:

```
stmt:
    CALL ident '(' expr ')' {
        $stmt = call_func($ident, $expr);
    }
```

Finally, note that named references are still considered experimental, but I am still including them because they are so helpful for readability.

3.4.9 Supporting divergent input versions

Everything changes over time, and there is an unavoidable possibility that your language will as well. For example, a hypothetical "version 2" of some language may allow the following:

```
print "foo";
```

Whereas a "version 3" may suddenly have parentheses:

```
print("foo");
```

Even though the assignment statement (and many others!) did not change:

```
myvar = "str";
```

If you are lucky enough that your language requires a version declaration as the first element (e.g. a custom database format), then one approach to resolve this is to encode all possibilities in your grammar and let the version value determine which path to take. For this to work best, it helps to have Flex return a different token for each version, so here is one possibility:

```
    // Flex:
version[ \t]+2 { return VERSION2; }
version[ \t]+3 { return VERSION3; }

    // Bison:
top:
  VERSION2 v2_stmts
  | VERSION3 v3_stmts
  ;

v2_stmts:
  %empty
  | v2_stmts v2_print
  | v2_stmts common_assign
  ;

v3_stmts:
  %empty
  | v3_stmts v3_print
  | v3_stmts common_assign
  ;

common_assign:
  ID '=' STR ';' ;

v2_print:
  PRINT STR ';' ;

v3_print:
  PRINT '(' STR ')' ';' ;
```

This would allow either "version 2" input:

```
version 2
print "foo";
myvar = "foo";
```

Or "version 3" input:

```
version 3
print("foo");
myvar = "foo";
```

This approach works (and it even throws errors in the right place, despite there being rules matching "incorrect" syntax), but there are some caveats. First is that requiring a version string at the beginning of any input would be a nonstarter for many grammars, especially if the format has been widely used before this question arose. A second issue is that every divergent point in the grammars will create a new rule, which bloats the parser's memory footprint and runtime with inherently unused rules.

A second approach is to split the grammars completely and compile them separately. For this, remember to specify name prefixes so that the parsers do not collide (%option prefix and %define api.prefix). The messy part, however, is that you also need a runtime way to determine which grammar to use. Some (third) parser is necessary just to determine the version number, but you have to be careful to ignore everything else since you do not yet know how to parse it. You can see why XML requires that if a file declares a version, that declaration must start on the first line of the file:

```
<?xml version = "1.0"?>
```

Splitting the grammars like this results in code duplication of all the rules that did not change (e.g. our common_assign above), but an argument could be made that it is redeemed by the corresponding lack of coupling between the parsers.

3.5 Gotchas

3.5.1 Use GLR only as a last resort

When Bison's one symbol of lookahead is insufficient to handle a particular grammar, you can turn on GLR (Generalized Left-Right[45]) mode. GLR is the ten-ton-hammer approach; when it encounters a situation it cannot resolve with one token of lookahead, it spawns copies of the parser and tries each possible parse in parallel. When one of the copies encounters a parse error, that copy is destroyed. The last one left standing is the final parse.

GLRs can handle any unambiguous grammar, regardless of the number of tokens needed to disambiguate. There are situations where GLRs are the only solution, but there are some considerations to keep in mind before you start using it all the time:
 • GLRs may split unnecessarily. Check Bison's reported conflicts by running with -v to make sure it is resorting to a GLR only when it really needs to. You may be able to use some of the conflict-resolution tricks to avoid the GLR split.
 • If your grammar is truly ambiguous, then the split done by the GLR will require handholding to merge. See section 1.5.2 of the Bison manual for details on how to use %dprec in that situation.
 • GLR does not work well with Flex states. Since Bison consumes tokens but does not execute user actions until a single parse path is established, you may easily run into issues controlling Flex's start-states at the appropriate times.
 • Typically, GLR incurs only a minor speed

---

[45] As opposed to Bison's usual LALR (Look-Ahead Left-Right).

degradation, but in the worst pathological cases it can take cubic time and space.

See the "GLR Parsing" section of chapter 9 of *Flex & Bison* for a great summary on using GLRs, and section 1.5 of the Bison manual for full details.

3.5.2 Use pure parsers for reentrancy

By default, Bison's parsers are not reentrant, but only for historical reasons. Bison will generate reentrant parsers by turning on what it calls "pure" parsing. The core idea is to move all the global variables into `structs` so that we have a "lexer object" and a "parser object" with encapsulated data. This, in turn, will change the interfaces of most of the functions we use.

Though there is almost no performance penalty for enabling pure parsing, this is a retrofitted feature that is not particularly straightforward, so the syntax for getting this to work changes dramatically depending on which versions of both Flex and Bison you use. As of this writing, my reluctant recommendation is to try this only if you truly need reentrancy. It is somewhat risky to start a new parser with reentrancy because subsequent versions of Flex and Bison might make this mechanism much easier.

The changes to the Flex source are blissfully minimal:
- Add `%option reentrant`, to bundle the lexer's global variables into a `struct`.
- Add `%option bison-bridge`, which adjusts the definition of `yylex` to minimize changes to Bison's invocation.

The changes to the Bison source are much more invasive:
- Add `%define api.pure full` to bundle the parser's globals into a `struct`. (There used to be a

`%pure-parser`, but that is deprecated.)[46]

• Define `yyscan_t` as a `typedef` of `void*`. We are actually *re*defining it (it is part of Flex's output), but we cannot use `extern` for a `typedef`, and Flex does not generate a header that Bison can use[47].

• Add an extern declaration for `yyset_in`, because we can no longer set `yyin` directly.

• Add extern declarations for `yylex_init` and `yylex_destroy`, which are the constructor and destructor functions for `yyscan_t` objects.

• Update the declaration and definition of `yyerror` to include a new first argument of `yyscan_t`.

• Pass a `yyscan_t` object to `yylex`, with `%lex-param`.

• Pass a `yyscan_t` object to `yyparse`, with `%parse-param`.

There are also changes needed to the program's invocation of the parser:

• Create a `yyscan_t` object.

• Call `yylex_init` to initialize the `yyscan_t` object.

• Call `yyset_in` instead of setting `yyin` directly, because `yyin` is no longer a global variable.

• Call `yyparse` (or `yylex`, if you are only scanning) with the `yyscan_t` object.

• Call `yylex_destroy` to clean up the `yyscan_t` object.

---

[46] Historical note: `true` used to be a valid value for `%define api.pure`, to say that pure parsing should be enabled. However, that was deprecated in favor of `full` in version 2.6.90 in order to add a locations parameter to `yyerror`.

[47] Well, it *can*, but this creates a dependency loop with both Flex and Bison wanting the other's header file.

Here is a minimal example showing how to get it to work. I echo *Flex & Bison*'s suggestion that you should first check to see if more recent versions of Flex and Bison have simplified this mechanism.

```
// Flex:
%option reentrant
%option bison-bridge
%%
...


// Bison:
%{
  typedef void* yyscan_t;
  void yyerror(yyscan_t, const char *);
%}

%define api.pure full
%lex-param {yyscan_t this_scanner}
%parse-param {yyscan_t this_scanner}
...


// Program:
typedef void* yyscan_t;
extern void yyset_in(FILE*, yyscan_t);
extern int yylex(YYSTYPE*, yyscan_t);
extern int yylex_init(yyscan_t*);
extern int yylex_destroy(yyscan_t);
extern int yyparse(yyscan_t);

int main(int, char**) {

  yyscan_t myscanner;
  if (yylex_init(&myscanner)) {
    printf("ERROR during init");
    return -1;
  }
  yyparse(myscanner);
  yylex_destroy(myscanner);
```

```
        }

int yyerror(yyscan_t this_scanner,
    char *errmsg) {
  ...
}
```

(If you put your program code into the Bison file,
then some of the declarations have an ordering
dependency on YYSTYPE. To get that to work, I had to put
the typedef of yyscan_t in a %code top block, while
leaving everything else in a %code block.)

Also note that there is interaction between enabling
pure parsers and using locations. See §3.2.5 ("Dealing
with %locations") for full details.

For other perspectives, see section 9 of the Flex
manual, and section 3.7.10 of the Bison manual. Especially
see the first half of chapter 9 of *Flex & Bison* for John
Levine's approach to getting reentrant Flex working with
reentrant Bison.

3.5.3 Do not use $0, $-1, etc

In addition to the $1, $2, etc. variables that hold
the values for each token in a rule, Bison also has $0, $-1,
etc. variables for referencing values of *previous* tokens in
the parent rule. An example:

```
foo:
    thing1 bar
    | thing2 bar ;

bar:
    thing3 { $$ = $0; } ;
```

The value of the bar token is set to the value of
either the thing1 or thing2 token, depending on the
input.

While this isolated testcase works fine, the
dependency that bar now has on its context makes the
grammar much more fragile. Any new use of bar would
need to ensure that its context satisfies an unobvious
assumption. Worse, any change to either the definition or
consumption of bar has to be verified on a larger scale
than usual.

A significant part of the maintenance burden is its
readability. If the code owner discovered bar by seeing its
definition, there is a chance they would read $0 as the first
token value (and why not — C has an established history
of starting arrays at 0 instead of 1). $0 et al are not
sufficiently common that their semantics should be
assumed.

However, if the owner discovered bar from its use
in foo, then we have another problem — there is no
indication in foo's rule that bar has a context dependency.

A copy-paste update has a good risk of going horribly wrong.

On balance, try to avoid $0 et al so as to try to avoid a possible maintenance nightmare.

3.6 Development & Debugging

3.6.1 Use `%define parse.trace` and `yydebug`

Bison has the ability to print out debugging messages to show you what it is doing. This is immensely useful because normal debugging techniques (such as `gdb` and `print` statements) are somewhat less than effective; Bison is, after all, just simulating a state machine. Bison's debugging messages indicate three things:

- what tokens it receives from Flex,
- the contents of the token stack after every shift and reduce, and
- which rules are used on each reduction

Enabling these message involves two steps. The first step (which applies at compile-time) is to have Bison build the parser with tracing enabled, which you do with `%define parse.trace`[48]. The second step (which applies at run-time) is to turn the messages on by setting `yydebug` to a nonzero value before calling `yyparse`. Since you cannot recompile deployed code, it is suggested you always build with `%define parse.trace`, and use some mechanism (a `-v` or a `--debug` command line switch, perhaps) to set `yydebug` only when needed.

The generated messages are quite verbose, in order to be helpful for finding a variety of possible problems. For this trivial grammar:

```
%%
top: FOO BAR ;
```

---

[48] This is a Bison extension that supplants the old `%debug` directive.

It generates the following:

```
Starting parse
Entering state 0
Reading a token: Next token is token FOO ()
Shifting token FOO ()
Entering state 1
Reading a token: Next token is token BAR ()
Shifting token BAR ()
Entering state 3
Reducing stack by rule 1 (line 19):
   $1 = token FOO ()
   $2 = token BAR ()
-> $$ = nterm top ()
Stack now 0
Entering state 2
Reading a token: Now at end of input.
Shifting token $end ()
Entering state 4
Stack now 0 2 4
Cleanup: popping token $end ()
Cleanup: popping nterm top ()
```

As soon as you try to use this to do actual
debugging, you will immediately notice that while it prints
out symbol *names*, it does not print out their *values,* and
those are potentially very interesting. Bison cannot print
them in general because they could be any arbitrary type,
but to help it along you can define your own code to print
out the values of each token type. This is the special
%printer directive:

```
%union {
  int ival;
  char *sval;
}

%token <ival>FOO
%token <sval>BAR

%printer {
  fprintf(yyoutput, "%i", $$);
} <ival>

%printer {
  fprintf(yyoutput, "%s", $$);
} <sval>
```

Then the debug output includes the token values in those parentheses that were empty in our last run:

```
Reading a token: Next token is token FOO
(42)
  Shifting token FOO (42)
  …
Reading a token: Next token is token BAR
(mystr)
  Shifting token BAR (mystr)
```

3.6.2 Avoid trying to perfectly handle unordered lists

Suppose you have some language construct that has unique optional elements, and they may appear in any order. As a contrived example, consider parsing a command line that may have -a, -b, and/or -c switches, in any order, but each should be specified at most once.

To correctly parse an unordered list using only grammar rules, you would have to enumerate every legal combination. If we made rules for our switches named opt_A, opt_B, and opt_C for the above, then all of the valid combinations would be:

```
%empty
opt_A
opt_B
opt_C
opt_A opt_B
opt_B opt_A
opt_A opt_C
opt_C opt_A
opt_B opt_C
opt_C opt_B
opt_A opt_B opt_C
opt_A opt_C opt_B
opt_B opt_A opt_C
opt_B opt_C opt_A
opt_C opt_A opt_B
opt_C opt_B opt_A
```

Implementing your grammar like this is obviously pretty painful, and it gets exponentially worse as you increase the number of items.

To avoid this, you can relax the grammar's enforcement of the uniqueness requirement. This makes the grammar substantially more straightforward by pushing the uniqueness check elsewhere[49]:

```
options:
  %empty
  | options opt_A
  | options opt_B
  | options opt_C
  ;
```

Now we can add our own uniqueness check:

```
%{
int specified_A = 0;
int specified_B = 0;
int specified_C = 0;
%}

%%
options:
  %empty
  | options opt_A {
    if (specified_A)
      yyerror("more than one -a!");
    specified_A = 1;
  }
  | options opt_B {
    if (specified_B)
      yyerror("more than one -b!");
    specified_B = 1;
  }
  | options opt_C {
    if (specified_C)
      yyerror("more than one -c!");
    specified_C = 1;
  }
%%
```

---

[49] Academically, this does not recognize the same language. However, we will check for uniqueness on our own, so the final result will be equivalent.

As these are global state variables, remember to reset them if your input could have more than one of these lists.

3.6.3 Turn on %verbose for debugging

The %verbose directive (which is equivalent to the -v/--verbose command-line switches) generates an extra file that shows you what each parse state does on each input. The file is created alongside your foo.tab.c file as foo.output (unless you redirect it with --report-file).

A second way to generate the .output file is with --report, which lets you pick and choose which kinds of things to include. %verbose is equivalent to running with --report=all, but you can restrict it to just the state descriptions (state), state transitions (itemset), lookahead symbols (lookahead), or the rules that had conflicts that were successfully resolved with precedence and associativity (solved).

For a full walkthrough of the .output file, see §3.1.5 ("Reading conflict messages"), and section 8.1 of the Bison manual.

3.6.4 Testing individual rules

One complexity with testing Bison rules is isolation — sometimes the one small piece you want to check exists only buried under many other rules. An example might be math expressions, which are expected as part of assignment but not as a standalone element:

```
top:
  stmts
  ;

stmts: %empty | stmts stmt ;

stmt: assign ;

assign: ID '=' math_expr ;

math_expr:
  ID
  | math_expr '+' math_expr
  | math_expr '-' math_expr
  | math_expr '*' math_expr
  | math_expr '/' math_expr ;
```

To test such rules, one approach is to add a "test backdoor" to your top rule, with the net effect of reducing the expected input to just that one rule:

```
top:
  stmts
  | TEST_EXPR math_expr
  | TEST_ASSIGN assign
  ;
  ...
```

Then, you can create a phony marker token at the beginning of your input, and have Flex return phony corresponding TEST_EXPR or TEST_ASSIGN tokens:

```
__test_expr__    {
    return TEST_EXPR;
}
__test_assign__    {
    return TEST_ASSIGN;
}
```

This enables a project to have isolated input files for a given rule, allowing specific targeting for unit tests and regressions:

```
% cat math_expr.input
__test_expr__  a + a - a * a / a
```

If requiring __test_expr__ in the input is undesirable, another approach is to manually override the first token returned by yylex. This approach uses a global variable in a *rules*[50] section code block to exit out of yylex early:

---

50 This is the second section of the file, after the first %%

```
    // Flex:
%{
int override_token = 0;
%}
…
%%
%{
  if (override_token) {
    int t = override_token;
    override_token = 0;
    return t;
  }
%}
…


    // Program:
extern int override_token;
override_token = TEST_EXPR;
yyparse();
```

3.7 Speed

3.7.1 Minimize the number of rules

In general, having more rules slows parsing down, and also (slightly) increases the memory needed to hold the state tables. The degree to which your application can tolerate that is, of course, specific to your compute environment and constraints.

As an example, consider this silly grammar:

```
top: A B C D E F G ;
```

compared to this needlessly hierarchical equivalent:

```
top: r1 r2 ;
r1: A r3 ;
r2: E r4 ;
r3: r5 D ;
r4: F G ;
r5: B C ;
```

Even though they parse the exact same language, their generated state machines are completely different. The first one has 10 states whereas the second has 15. Each reduction has a runtime cost.

Another problem with having a lot of rules is that superfluous rules can introduce false conflicts. Consider:

```
top: A B C
   | A r1 C
   ;

r1: B ;
```

In this situation, B could either be reduced (to

satisfy r1) or shifted (to satisfy top), which introduces a shift/reduce conflict. However, in this example, there is effectively no reason to introduce the r1 rule.

3.7.2 Stop parsing as soon as you know you do not care about the rest of the input

There are some situations where you can save some time by stopping early. The most obvious one is if you hit a critical number of errors; especially because of cascaded errors, it is better to stop early than to spend time generating more errors that have a good chance of being misleading. Oddly, you cannot call YYABORT from within yyerror, because YYABORT is a goto to a label in yyparse, so instead you have to call exit (or abort) directly.

Another situation is when you want to parse only a section of a file. An example might be retrieving a single record from a text database — after you have read what you are looking for, you can call YYACCEPT to avoid unnecessarily parsing the remaining records.

Finally, some languages have an end-of-content marker, such as the __END__ section of perl scripts. __END__ specifies that the remainder of the file is to be used by the program as raw data, and so the parser could YYACCEPT as soon as it saw it.

3.8 Code Conventions

3.8.1 Write terminals in uppercase, nonterminals in lowercase

The use of case to distinguish between terminals and nonterminals is entirely a convention, but it is very well established. Even if the literal token text is lowercase (e.g. C's `for`), naming the token in uppercase (e.g. FOR) gives a clear visual cue in the grammar that greatly aids in readability:

```
stmt:
  if_stmt
  | for_stmt
  ;

if_stmt:
  IF '(' expr ')' THEN stmt opt_else
  ;

opt_else:
  %empty
  | ELSE stmt
  ;

for_stmt:
  FOR '(' expr ';' expr ';' expr ')'
  '{' stmts '}'
  ;
```

3.8.2 Use `%empty` to mark empty rules

Empty rules require no intentional marking, but a common convention for marking them is to add a comment:

```
items:
  /* empty */
| items one_item ;
```

However, Bison has a built-in mechanism for declaring empty rules: `%empty`

```
items:
  %empty
| items one_item ;
```

There are two advantages to `%empty`. First is the boost in readability. `%empty` is very obviously intentional, especially compared to grammars that do not even use comments to mark empty rules.

Second is that `-Wempty-rule` recognizes `%empty`, and limits warning to rules that are unintentionally empty. This warning is very helpful for catching stray `|` characters that unintentionally change the grammar:

```
top:
  // rule1: was deprecated
| rule2
| rule3
;
```

Here you can see the user commented out `rule1` when it was deprecated but forgot to remove the `|` between it and `rule2`.

3.8.3 Use directives instead of command-line flags

Bison lets you specify many options as either command-line flags or as directives. Of the two, the directives are (usually) preferable, because they keep the build parameters with the source code.

From a software architecture perspective, it makes more sense to couple Bison options with the Bison file than with the build environment. A change to a directive changes the source file, which definitely triggers a rebuild; a change to a command-line switch does not change the source file, so a rebuild would only be triggered if the makefile itself is dubiously added as a dependency.

One of the best candidate options is the name prefix. You could specify it with -p on the command-line, but using `%define api.prefix` inside the Bison file is much better.

However, there is one exception: the output file. It is best left as a command line switch (-o) instead of using either `%output` or `%file-prefix`. Implicit outputs introduce an element of mystery when trying to understand a build environment.

A helpful list of which command line switches have directives is in section 9.2 ("Option Cross Key") of the Bison manual.

3.8.4 Do not have multiple `%union`s

    `%union` allows you to define the elements of the union-type that `yylval` will be an instance of. As it turns out, Bison will let you declare multiple `%union` blocks, and it concatenates them all together:

```
%union {
   int ival;
   float fval;
}
%union {
   char *sval;
}
```

    However, this is *not* also true for C's `union`s. Once you declare a C `union`, you cannot append to it with a later declaration. Because of that difference, Bison's support for multiple `%union`s is highly unexpected. C programmers will expect that the first `%union` contains all the information they need to know. Thus, including multiple `%union`s will make your source more difficult to navigate.

3.8.5 Define a nonterminal only once

There are two ways to specify an "or"-type relation in a rule: use the pipe character (" | ") within a single rule, or define a nonterminal in multiple rules. The following are equivalent:

```
// Using pipe:
A_or_B: A | B ;

// Using multiple rules:
A_or_B: A ;
A_or_B: B ;
```

Even though they are functionally equivalent, using a pipe is preferable. For one reason, the intent of " | " is immediately clear, whereas multiple definitions of a nonterminal could be resolved as last-one-wins. (Or as first-one-wins. Neither is true, but the fact that there is ambiguity is the point.)

Additionally, defining a nonterminal only once reduces your risk of typos, since there are fewer mentions of the literal text A_or_B. Similarly, it lowers your maintenance burden should you ever rename it.

Worst though, there is no requirement that multiple definitions of a given nonterminal be adjacent. Thus, there is nothing preventing anyone from distributing them widely across the grammar, making it unnecessarily obfuscated.

3.8.6 Use `%param` to avoid global variables

Since Flex and Bison predate object-oriented programming, global variables are fairly common. In addition to polluting the global namespace, globals are problematic if your parser needs to be either recursive or multi-threaded. You may have already enabled pure parsing to avoid Flex's and Bison's global variables (see §3.5.2, "Use pure parsers for reentrancy"), but there is still the problem of how to use your own objects inside Bison code blocks.

The `%param` directive allows you to add custom parameters to `yylex` and `yyparse` for your own use:

```
// Bison:
%param {int foo} {int *bar}
%%
%%

// Program:
int A, B;
yyparse(A, &B);
```

Inside `yyparse` (and hence inside all of your grammar's code blocks) you now have access to the `foo` and `bar` variables.

Note that if you enabled pure parsing, your custom `%param` variables are added to the end of the list of `yyparse`'s arguments, after `YYSTYPE` (and `YYLTYPE`, if you also enabled `%locations`).

Helpfully, `%param` also adds these parameters to `yyerror`. However, unlike `yyparse`, it adds the parameters to the beginning of `yyerror`'s arguments. The above example would expect `yyerror` to have this signature:

```
void yyerror(int, int*, const char*);
```

And if you have enabled %locations, yyerror's signature would turn into this:

```
void yyerror(int, int*, YYLTYPE*, const char*);
```

3.8.7 Put initialization code into %initial-action

Each time yyparse is called, Bison invokes any code you put in an %initial-action block, making it a great place to put nontrivial initialization code. In particular, since the code is inserted at the beginning of yyparse, it has access to any custom %param and %parse-param variables, whereas usual %code blocks do not.

Note that %initial-action is not helpful for declaring additional variables — they will not be visible in your rules, because the code is lexically scoped in a { ... } block.

As a trivial example, consider a database object that should be reset before your parser populates it. You could call a reset_data function before every invocation of yyparse, or you could factor it out into a single %initial-action block:

```
%parse-param { struct DB *local_db }
%initial-action {
  reset_data(local_db, current_time);
}
```

3.8.8 Use `%code{ ... }` instead of `%{ ... %}`

`%code{ ... }` is Bison's update to Yacc's `%{ ... %}`. It is more than a syntax change - it also allows you to specify a qualifier as to where the code should go, which is important when the code either requires definitions from or supplies definitions to Bison-generated code.

The first block copied to the Bison output is from `%code top`. It is placed after a handful of constant `#define`s such as `YYBISON_VERSION`.[51]

Immediately following it is the code from a legacy `%{ ... %}` block. `%code top` is meant to replace the anonymous code block, but you if still have both, this is their ordering.

The `%code requires` block is next, after a few more `#define`s resolving the values of `YY_NULLPTR`, `YYERROR_VERBOSE`, and `YYDEBUG`. Since the latter controls the existence of the declaration of `yydebug`, this is the earliest you would want to include any code that references it. More importantly, this is the last block before `YYSTYPE` and `YYLTYPE` are defined, so this is a good place in which to declare any types used in your `%union` directive. Note that this block is printed to *both* the `tab.c` and `tab.h` files (unlike any of the previous blocks, which go to only the `tab.c` file), so be careful about including definitions vs. declarations.

The next block comes from `%code provides`. Since it is after the definitions of `YYSTYPE` and `YYLTYPE`,

---

[51] Note: `%code` goes to a different locations for Java output; I continue assuming C usage. Java also has a `%code imports` that C output does not have.

this is usually the best place to put everything else, some of which needs those definitions. `%code provides` blocks are also printed to both `tab.c` and `tab.h`.

The last block is the unqualified `%code`, which immediately follows.

At the very least, you should use `%code` instead of a bare legacy `%{...%}`. Even though the legacy usage is very established, `%code` is a clear win for readability.

Here is an example, distilled from section 3.1.2 of the Bison manual, showing intended semantics and best practice for these different blocks:

```
%code top {
// Global header files.
#include <stdio.h>
}

%code requires {
// Headers and declarations needed
// for YYSTYPE (%union).
#include "mytype.h"
}

%union {
  long itype;
  struct mytype otype;
}

%code provides {
// Declarations of things that use
// YYSTYPE or YYLTYPE, and/or should be
// visible to both the parser and
// external consumers.
extern int yylex(YYSTYPE*, YYLTYPE*);[52]
}

%code {
// Declarations of things that use
// YYSTYPE or YYLTYPE, but do not need
// to be visible outside of the parser.
static int yyerror(YYLTYPE*,
    const char*);
}
```

---

[52] Assuming you have turned on locations and pure parsing.

3.8.9 Declare a name prefix

Even using a pure parser, Flex and Bison communicate through global identifiers, with `yylex` being a particularly important one. There is a collision hazard with these identifiers when using multiple parsers in a single program. In fact, even if *your* program is not using multiple parsers, someone else may want to include your parser in a program that has another Bison parser.

The resolution is to declare a name prefix, which Flex and Bison will use instead of `yy` or `YY` in all of their visible functions and variables. For example, to use `foo_` instead of `yy`, include the following in your Bison source:

```
%define api.prefix {foo_}
```

And correspondingly rename Flex's identifiers in its source:

```
%option prefix="foo_"
```

This changes the names of `yylex` and `yyparse` to `foo_lex` and `foo_parse`. The full list of Bison identifiers affected by the name change is:
- `yyparse`
- `yyerror`
- `yydebug`
- `yynerrs`
- `yylval`
- `yychar`

There are even more Flex identifiers affected:
- `yylex`
- `yyin`
- `yyleng`
- `yyout`
- `yyrestart`

- `yytext`
- `yywrap`
- `yyalloc/yyrealloc/yyfree`
- all of the various buffer functions (`yy_create_buffer`, `yy_push_buffer_state`, etc).

Due to the scope of the impact, this is obviously a change best made near the beginning of the project.

Appendix A: A somewhat quick overview of parsing theory

Knowing the details of how parsing works in Flex and Bison may or may not contribute to your skills using them. However, for true geeks, knowing this stuff is great conversation material for the cocktail parties we never get invited to.

Like many computer science problems, parsing was approached with divide-and-conquer. In order to recognize patterned input, the stream of input characters is first lexed into atomic units that identify their role ("tokens", though their true academic name is "lexemes"), and then the tokens are grouped ("parsed") according to rules that relate those roles. Let's consider a simplified example: the ubiquitous mathematical expression:

```
1 + 2 * 3 - 4
```

There are two lexical elements in this example, with two roles: NUM (which we recognize as one or more digits) and OP (a plus sign, hyphen, or asterisk). After lexing, the input stream has been conceptually transformed into a stream of roles:

input stream	token stream
1	NUM
+	OP
2	NUM
*	OP
3	NUM
-	OP
4	NUM

Next, the roles are then parsed by matching them with patterns from a grammar. For this example we will define two grammatical elements: `expr` matching a single NUM, and `expr` matching the recursive three-element sequence "expr OP expr":

```
expr ::= NUM
expr ::= expr OP expr
```

With these, we can match up the stream of tokens with our grammar. There are many ways we could match these two rule to this stream of tokens. Here, I present a bad way to do it.

By rule 1, all NUMs are exprs, so the stream becomes:

input	token	pass1
1	NUM	expr
+	OP	OP
2	NUM	expr
*	OP	OP
3	NUM	expr
+	OP	OP
4	NUM	expr

By rule 2, we can collapse any "`expr OP expr`" sequence down to just `expr`:

input	token	pass1	pass2
1	NUM	expr	
+	OP	OP	expr
2	NUM	expr	
*	OP	OP	OP
3	NUM	expr	
+	OP	OP	expr
4	NUM	expr	

And we can do it again on the result to reduce the whole thing down to a single `expr`:

input	token	pass1	pass2	pass3
1	NUM	expr		
+	OP	OP	expr	
2	NUM	expr		
*	OP	OP	OP	expr
3	NUM	expr		
+	OP	OP	expr	
4	NUM	expr		

The result is that we know that the given input exactly matches our definition of `expr`.

This example shows the basics of the theory, but in practice there are complexities. First, our input expression contained whitespace (spaces, tabs, newlines) but there was no handling for that in either phase. (Typically, phase one recognizes whitespace with a specific pattern, but does not actually report it to phase two.) Another complexity is that our grammar is ambiguous -- there are multiple ways to match this token stream against these grammar rules. The way we did it in this example is horrendous because we inverted algebraic precedence. "1+2*3+4" should be matched like "1+(2*3)+4", but we matched it like "(1+2)*(3+4)". This is why parsers need to understand precedence and associativity.

These two phases are implemented respectively by Flex (raw input to tokens) and Bison (tokens to patterns).

They seem similar: both phases essentially match an input stream against a set of patterns. However, they differ in complexity. File formats (or more correctly, *languages*) have degrees of complexity, and theorists classify them according to how powerful a parser you need to understand them. Bison deals with what are called *context-free languages,* and Flex with *regular languages.*

At a lower level, there is also an implementation difference: lexing must use a queue (because it has to include the head of its input stream), but LR parsing must use a stack (because nesting requires matching the tail of the stream).

Context-Free Languages

Context-free languages (CFLs) recognize recursive sequences, and the specification of a context-free language is called a grammar. The sequences (rules) are hierarchical, and so can contain any mixture of low-level tokens and other rules. The expr example we used above shows a CFL, so let's continue with it:

```
expr ::=
        NUM
        | STRING
        | expr OP expr
        | "(" expr ")"
        | "-" expr
        ;
```

This defines a rule named expr that can match any of five different sequences. The first sequence recognizes a numeric constant; the second recognizes a text string that we will semantically interpret as a variable name. The others all recognize sequences containing sub-expressions, allowing us to build arbitrarily complex expressions.

Of particular note is that the above definition will recognize nested parentheses. That is, it can validate the correctness of "(((((4)))))" and the incorrectness of "(4)))".

CFLs can be parsed by using a state machine and a stack. As each low-level token is pushed onto the stack, the parser changes its state, and the top tokens on the stack are checked against whatever grammar rules correspond to that state. If there is a match, those tokens are removed from the stack and replaced by a token representing that rule. When there is no more input, the stack ideally contains the single token representing the highest-level rule of the grammar, indicating that the input stream matches the given language.

There is some terminology to cover at this point, so that you can understand Bison's error messages. In the parsing world, they do not say that a token is *pushed* onto the stack, they say that it is *shifted* onto the stack. Then, the inverse process of removing tokens from the stack and replacing them with another token is called *reducing*, presumably because it (usually) reduces the size of the stack. For consistency with the tools, I will use *shift* and *reduce*.

Example

As an example, let's consider a deceptively simple assignment statement:

```
x := y+z*3+2
```

The grammar rules are:

```
%left '+'
%left '*'

assignment: lvalue ASSIGN expr ;
expr:       NUMBER ;
expr:       variable ;
expr:       expr '+' expr ;
expr:       expr '*' expr ;
variable:   STRING ;
lvalue:     variable ;
```

First, let's convert the raw input into its corresponding tokens. Since the intent of this example is to show how the parser works, let's assume the lexing phase without going into details:

input	*tokens*
x	STRING
:=	ASSIGN
y	STRING
+	'+'
z	STRING
*	'*'
3	NUM
+	'+'
2	NUM

Then we start shifting tokens onto the stack:

```
stack: STRING
```

We check our grammar rules to see if any of them match the stack, and we see that we can reduce STRING to variable:

```
stack: variable
```

Checking the new stack, we see that we now have two other rules that could further reduce: lvalue and expression can both replace a variable. How do we know which one to choose? This is a reduce/reduce conflict, because there is more than one possible reduction. Which one we choose depends on our state. At the very beginning of the input, we are looking for lvalue, so we clearly choose that reduction:

```
stack: lvalue
```

We do not see anything else to do, so we shift the next token (ASSIGN) onto the stack:

```
stack: lvalue ASSIGN
```

We find we still have nothing to do, so we shift the next token (STRING):

```
stack: lvalue ASSIGN STRING
```

We see that we can perform another STRING-to-variable reduction, giving us:

```
stack: lvalue ASSIGN variable
```

But now we have the same problem we had earlier: do we reduce variable to expression or to lvalue? It so happens that we know lvalue is only valid as the very first token, so we want to reduce this variable to expression. This is another piece of information that came from our state machine:

```
stack: lvalue ASSIGN expression
```

And we find ourselves with a new problem. The stack now matches assignment (perfectly, actually), so we could reduce the whole stack down to it. However, we still have input to shift on the stack, and our language does not accept "assignment with stuff after it," so what do we do? This is what is called a shift/reduce conflict, where we could either shift more stuff onto the stack in anticipation of matching a bigger rule, or reduce now to

207

match what we have. This is also resolved through the use of the state machine, but much of time it turns out that both the shift and the reduce are valid, so it is not always easy to figure out. Notice though that we know the next piece of input is +, which could eventually match `expression`. In that case, our action will be to prefer the shift over the reduce. (And that is what Bison will do.) After shifting + onto the stack we have:

```
stack: lvalue ASSIGN expression '+'
```

which matches nothing, so we shift the next token (a `STRING`) to get:

```
stack: lvalue ASSIGN expression '+'
STRING
```

By now you should already mechanically know what we are doing next: reducing `STRING` to `variable` and then to `expression`, giving us:

```
stack: lvalue ASSIGN expression '+'
expression
```

Now we get all excited because we see that the "`expression` + `expression`" can reduce down to just `expression`, but we are stopped short but yet another shift-reduce conflict. Since the top of the stack (an `expression`) matches the beginning of a rule (both "`expression` + `expression`" and "`expression` * `expression`"), we may have to keep shifting for a future reduction instead of taking the one we have now. However, it gets even nastier, because here in the real world we need it to respect algebraic precedence and associativity as well.

Aren't you glad you are not doing this by hand?

The state machine cannot help us with this one — what we want to do next completely depends on the next token of input. If we see +, the input is looking like "a+b+c", and the associativity rule for addition says we have to group left to right (that is, "(a+b)+c", not "a+(b+c)"..which does not make one whit of difference for addition but it would for subtraction). In that case, we want to reduce the "expression + expression" at the top of the stack down to just expression, and carry on.

However, if the next token is *, the input is looking like "a+b*c", and the precedence rule for multiplication says we have to multiply before we add (that is, "a+(b*c)", not "(a+b)*c"). Then, we want to shift instead of reduce.

We see that the next token is indeed *, so we continue shifting to get:

```
stack: lvalue ASSIGN expression '+'
expression '*'
```

and shift again to get:

```
stack: lvalue ASSIGN expression '+'
expression '*' NUMBER
```

NUMBER can be reduced down to expression, so we go ahead and do that:

```
stack: lvalue ASSIGN expression '+'
expression '*' expression
```

And again we find ourselves in a position where we could either shift or reduce. However, this situation is not quite so pathological. If the next token is +, then the precedence of multiplication would make us reduce instead of shift; if the next token is *, then the associativity of multiplication (left-to-right) would also make us reduce instead of shift. Thus we know we have to reduce, giving us:

```
stack: lvalue ASSIGN expression '+'
expression
```

Well this is familiar, and all the previous logic holds, except now our next token is + instead of *. That means the relevant rule for choosing between shift or reduce is the associativity of +. Since it is left to right, we choose reducing over shifting, the opposite of what we did last time:

```
stack: lvalue ASSIGN expression
```

This is also familiar, and for the same reasons we again decide to prefer the shift over the reduce to get:

```
stack: lvalue ASSIGN expression '+'
```

One final shift finishes our input:

```
stack: lvalue ASSIGN expression '+'
NUMBER
```

NUMBER reduces to expression:

```
stack: lvalue ASSIGN expression '+'
expression
```

The lack of a next token means we now always prefer reducing over shifting (because there is nothing to shift!), so we reduce to get:

```
stack: lvalue ASSIGN expression
```

With that same logic, we again reduce:

```
stack: assignment
```

And we are left with the stack containing the top-level token. Done!

Regular Languages

Regular languages identify non-recursive sequences, and the specification of a regular language is called a *regular expression*. For our purposes (lexing), our input is a stream of characters, so for us regular expressions are just strings of text with control characters. Here are the control modifiers recognized by Flex:

control modifier	description	example	patterns matched
.	matches any single character that is not a carriage return	a.c	aac, abc, acc, adc, ...
*	matches the previous item any number of times	ab*	a, ab, abb, abbb, ...
+	matches the previous item at least once	ab+	ab, abb, abbb, ...
?	matches the previous item zero or one time	ab?	a, ab
[]	matches any one character listed between the brackets	a[bcd]	ab, ac, ad
{n,m}	matches the previous item between n and m times (inclusive)	a{2,4}	aa, aaa, aaaa
|	matches items on either side	abc|def	abc, def
/	matches the first pattern only if it is followed by the second pattern	abc/def	abcdef

Regular languages can recognize tons of patterns, but because they have no recursion they have no memory: you cannot write a regex that validates nested parentheses. For this reason, regular languages are considered weaker than context-free languages. There are still two good reasons for using them though: first, they are good enough for lexing; second, simpler code runs faster.

Example

As an example, let's match some identifiers, numbers, keywords, and whitespace. Here are our patterns:

```
[ \t]+                     ;

while                    { return WHILE; }
for                      { return FOR; }
foreach                  { return
FOREACH; }
    [0-9]+               { return NUMBER; }
    [a-zA-Z][a-zA-Z0-9]* { return
IDENTIFIER; }
```

Each of these patterns can be turned into a state machine, and the six resulting state machines can be combined into one. Lexing works (conceptually) by feeding the input characters into the state machine until there is only a single possible match.

Suppose we give it this input:

```
while food
```

There are 6 patterns, so at the very start there are 6 possible matches; after seeing the w character there are only two (while and identifier). For the next four characters (hile), the input continues to match both while and identifier. The sixth character (a space) does not match either rule. Since the rules stopped after the same number of characters, the way to choose which rule is selected is by preferring the one listed first in the list of patterns. Since while is listed before identifier, it matches while.

Now we are on the 6th character. There is only one rule that matches an initial space, so we just scan forward to make the biggest match possible. An action is not specified for this rule, so the lexer does nothing with this token, and just resumes looking for the next token.

On the 7th character, we have an f. That matches three rules: for, foreach, and identifier. The next character (o) also matches all three, but the next after that (o) only matches identifier. We now know which rule will get returned, but we have to continue matching as much as we can. After we read the d we hit the end of input, so we are done matching.

Now let's try something more pathological by taking out the identifier rule and giving it the input foreacj. The first three characters match for and foreach. At the fourth character we no longer match for, but we cannot just assume that the rest of the input is necessarily going to match foreach. We have to remember that we matched for but keep going. For the next three characters (eac) we continue matching foreach, but at the 7th character (j), we no longer match foreach. We return the last rule we did match (for), and the next token will start at the e.

This example shows part of the broader problem of matching patterns greedily -- since we have to match the longest possible text, we essentially have to trace until no patterns match, and then back up to the last one that did.

Appendix B: full `#include` example

This is a Flex-only implementation of C's `#include` mechanism as discussed in §2.4.7. This implementation keeps track of the state of the input buffer, the file name, the line number, and the start-state.

```
%{
struct bufstackstr {
    // This stack is implemented as a
    // linked list:
    struct bufstackstr *prev;

    // YY_BUFFER_STATE is a typedef of a
    // pointer, so no asterisk here:
    YY_BUFFER_STATE buff;

    // Opened FILE object:
    FILE *file;

    // Name of file for this buffer:
    char *filename;

    // Line number, but (oddly) for
    // the previous buffer:
    int linenum;

    // Start-state, also for the
    // previous buffer:
    int startstate;
};

// Global buffer stack:
struct bufstackstr *bufstack=0;

// Declare our push_file function:
void mypush_file(const char *mypath);
```

```
%}

%array
%option stack
%option noyywrap

%x INCLUDE_QSTRING

%%

<*>[ \t]+  ; // Chomp whitespace

<INCLUDE_QSTRING>\"   {
    // (Borrowed from tip 3.4.4)
    yyleng = 0;   // overwrite quote char
    char ch;
    while ((ch = input()) && ch != 0) {
      // Handle an escape:
      if (ch == '\\') {
        ch = input();
        if (ch == 0); // error
        else {
          // No special treatment other
          // than to not add the escape
          // character to yytext:
          yytext[yyleng++] = ch;
        }
      }
      // End of string:
      else if (ch == '"') {
        // Overwrite quote char with
        // the end-of-string marker:
        yytext[yyleng] = 0;
        break;
      }
      // Normal character:
      else {
        yytext[yyleng++] = ch;
      }
    }
    yy_pop_state();
    mypush_file(yytext);
```

```
    }

#include {
    yy_push_state(INCLUDE_QSTRING);
    }

<<EOF>> {[53]
    // Pop it from the custom stack:
    struct bufstackstr *popped_bufstack
        = bufstack;
    bufstack = bufstack->prev;

    // Close the file:
    fclose(popped_bufstack->file);

    // Delete the buffer:
    yy_delete_buffer(
        popped_bufstack->buff);

    // Clean up filename memory:
    free(popped_bufstack->filename);

    // Restore line number:
    yylineno = popped_bufstack->linenum;

    // Restore the start-state.  Do not
    // use BEGIN here!
    yy_start =
        popped_bufstack->startstate;

    // Delete the stack object memory:
    free(popped_bufstack);

    // If there's nothing more on the
    // stack, then are done with
    // all input:
    if (!bufstack) return 0;
```

---

[53] You could put this block into a `mypop_file` function, for symmetry with `mypush_file`.

```
   // Switch buffer:
   yy_switch_to_buffer(bufstack->buff);
  }

\n      { ++yylineno; }
.|\n    { ECHO; }

%%

void mypush_file(const char *mypath) {

  // Open the file:
  FILE *myfile = fopen(mypath, "r");
  if (!myfile) {
    printf("ERROR\n");
    return;
  }

  // Create a buffer object:
  YY_BUFFER_STATE mybuff =
    yy_create_buffer(myfile,
    YY_BUF_SIZE);
  if (!mybuff) {
    printf("ERROR2\n");
    return;
  }

  // Create a stack frame:
  struct bufstackstr *mystackobj =
      malloc(
      sizeof(struct bufstackstr));
  mystackobj->buff = mybuff;
  mystackobj->file = myfile;
  mystackobj->filename = strdup(mypath);
  mystackobj->linenum = yylineno;
  mystackobj->startstate = yy_start;

  // Push it onto the stack:
  mystackobj->prev = bufstack;
  bufstack = mystackobj;
```

```
  // Reset yylineno for the new file:
  yylineno = 1;

  // New files start in INITIAL:
  BEGIN(INITIAL);

  // Switch yyin et al to the
  // new buffer:
  yy_switch_to_buffer(mybuff);
}

// A sample main to test:
int main() {

  mypush_file(argv[1]);

  while (yylex()) {
  }

  fclose(yyin);
  return 0;
}
```

Index

Trie ... 67

Made in the USA
Coppell, TX
17 January 2020